My Partial
Autobiography
with a Few Twists

Lessons
in
the Storm

Rita Polius Macon

Theological review and consultation provided by
Elder Ronnie D. Williams, Pastor

TEACH Services, Inc.
P U B L I S H I N G
www.TEACHServices.com • (800) 367-1844

Copyright © Rita Polius Macon
Copyright © 2014 TEACH Services, Inc.
ISBN-13: 978-1-4796-0293-3 (Paperback)
ISBN-13: 978-1-4796-0294-0 (ePub)
ISBN-13: 978-1-4796-0295-7 (Mobi)
Library of Congress Control Number: 2014909538

All scripture quotations are taken from the New American Standard Bible®.
Copyright © 1960, 1962, 1968, 1971, 1972, 1973, 1975, 1977, 1995 by The Lockman Foundation.
Used by permission.

Most names have been changed for privacy.

Published by

TEACH Services, Inc.
P U B L I S H I N G
www.TEACHServices.com • (800) 367-1844

Almost 27 years after my near-death automobile accident,
and approximately 42 years since my non-treatable
diagnosis by a physician.

"In repentance and rest you will be saved, in quietness and trust is your strength."
Isaiah 30:15

Dedication

I dedicate this book to two godly people: "My Sir," Mr. Bartholomew Gaspard, for his generosity and encouragement during my difficult past and the positive, ripple effects that his influence made on my life, and to Pastor Oscar Sherrod for his vision that made this manuscript possible.

Table of Contents

Chapter 1

———————

Why Lord?

The date was August 31, 1987. My husband and a friend carried me through the front door after an uncomfortable ride home from the hospital. I should be thankful that the automobile accident I experienced three months ago did not terminate my life; however, the long convalescence and slow progress toward recovery drained me.

As I lay on my back, trying not to cry from the excruciating pain in both my upper and lower lumbar regions, the words of my doctor rang in my head. "Recovery will be gradual for the first two and a half years ... some injuries are permanent."

My first thoughts during early recovery were those of brave determination: *I can fight this ... I have God on my side ... With God all things are possible... I cannot quit or lose because He is with me.*

Now, as I lay prostrate on my back, holding myself as still as possible in an effort to relieve the pain permeating my spinal cord, I feel more like a loser than a winner. My brave determination had since changed to questioning.

"Why, Lord?" I cried.

I have rejected the popular belief that Christians are to avoid questioning an omnipotent, omniscient God and trust that He will answer me. If only my stubborn, destructive self gave total submission to Divine guidance at all times, perhaps it would be easier to adhere to the unquestioning belief that God never makes a mistake and knows what is best for his children.

Unfortunately, I have a tendency to do wrong, like the apostle Paul, even though I truly desire to always do what is right. My pain was so real and unending that I felt I only had one choice –to inquire of the One who held my life in His hands. More than anything, I wanted my painful experience to be divinely appointed and not the result of suffering for my sins. If only I could be a chosen witness to bear testament to God's mercy in pain.

Am I undergoing Job's trial? I boldly asked myself.

"I don't think so," I replied aloud, shaking my head. Although Job's friends accused him of many faults, God, Himself, declared Job to be upright (Job 1:8). This witness alone indicates that the trials Job suffered through were not punitive justice on God's part.

When I was honest, I knew this was not the case with me. I am far from faultless. In fact, there is nothing about my life that I could compare with that of Job's. Deep down, I felt that instead of being placed on trial for my righteousness, I instead received a just form of chastisement for my constant rebellion. For a long time, I felt convicted that God had guided me to write the story of my life, and yet I lacked the will to submit and the conviction that my story would be worth the paper and ink.

Still, Hebrews 12:6 states, "For those whom the Lord loves He disciplines, and He scourges every son whom He receives." It seemed to me that a good father would not chastise his child without providing a reason for the chastisement. How could God chastise me for an unknown sin? My ignorance of the reason I had the accident made the punishment I felt I was experiencing seem contrary to the very character of God.

So, I continued to ask, "Why, Lord—why are You allowing me to exist in this state of discomfort and apprehension?" God had given us so much—a new address, the ability to establish a family business, the Medical Terminology Course certificate I was close to completing, and a new job that would help fund our family venture in its infancy. What good could I do for God by lying in bed, feeling helpless and deserted? I could even afford to help our church with its new mortgage. I wanted to know what disobedience on my part had led to my situation so that I could confess, repent, and reconcile.

In my distress, I lay sobbing. Although the physical pain I endured was part of the reason for my tears, the separation I felt from the One whom I firmly believed had stilled the storms of my life from birth was a much greater discomfort. Suddenly, in the middle of my agony, the present dilemma I was experiencing left my mind. In its place was a panoramic view of my past. Vividly, my early childhood captivated my attention.

The scene was St. Lucia, my island home arrayed with plenteous sunshine, hills and valleys, lush palm trees, and ever present children running, dancing and playing on the warm beaches. Catholicism is the primary religion of the island, as evidenced by LaCroix Maingot where a large cross rested on the peak of a hill across from a small chapel a short distance from my home in Bardinee.

The cross and chapel on the hill also mark the intersection of two roads. The northern road eventually led to a downhill pathway to my family home. The house itself was a large, four-room, framed house. There you would find older children busy with their daily chores among the happy laughter of younger children playing marbles or skipping rope. Occasionally, we paused from our work or play to listen to mother's conversations with the many adults walking the country road. Although instructed not to listen to their "grown people talk," it took the occasional lightning bolts shot at us from Mom's eyes to send us scrambling from her presence.

The setting alone should have ensured happy childhood for me. Although I was admired for my strength and courage even as a child, on the inside, I was filled with sorrow and anguish greater than what my heart wanted to bear. I believed that my courage made it easier for my family and friends to relate to me. It just did not seem fair to burden others with my problems and rob them of their happiness despite the fact that the need was always present to be authentic and cry in someone's arms. Thinking about the pity I would receive only served to enhance my distress.

However, communication with God was convenient. The dirt floor of an outhouse was our private meeting place. I knew He would not reveal my secrets to anyone. There, on my knees, I told God all my problems including my fears and doubts. In exchange, the comfort and peace He granted me assured confidence. This experience initiated my life of faith.

During this period, a small dark spot on the upper right side of my forehead that was originally identified as a simple birthmark grew throughout my early childhood and developed into an ugly mask of flesh. At the time, the inadequacies of medicine denied me an effective treatment. Therefore, many home remedies were applied in hopes of removing my unsightly blemish to no avail.

Then one day a promise of real help from the outside came in the form of a foreign doctor. Dr. Garrett was rumored to work medical wonders; many of those diagnosed with untreatable and inescapable maladies praised him for his effective remedies for their problems. He worked in the only hospital on the island, located in the main town of Castries. People streamed from every hill and valley on the island to visit with the "new doctor in town."

Appointments were mandatory, unless your disease was life threatening. The waiting list grew to such lengths that when you arrived on the scheduled date, you might wait all day in the crowded waiting area with little more to do than pray that your name would be among those called. If your prayers went unanswered, you would need to return the following day and continue your vigil. Some had to wait three or four days before finally being called. This wait did not deter those who brought their sick loved-ones to Dr. Garrett.

Although pregnant at the time, my mother took me. When I finally heard my name called, I was filled with elation. Just the thought of a normal face that would remove me from the center of attention seemed too good to be true. On the outside, I resorted to hiding behind my self-created mask of calmness and bravery. Inside, the questions and butterflies mounted: *Is this going to be the end of my problems? They say I look like my eldest sister, Martha, but will I truly look like her when I leave today? How can anyone say what I will look like after this mask is removed?*

Overwhelmed by everything, I leaned against my mother to reassure myself that I was not alone. It was then that I noticed she seemed more troubled and tired than usual, but I passed it off on her condition. As if reading my thoughts, she whispered, "It's going to be alright. God has finally answered our prayers."

These familiar words meant more to me than she would ever know. Throughout my ordeal, she had repeated them many times, such as after applying a new remedy recommended by well-meaning friends or family, or at night when she prayed with me. I wanted to tell her how I longed for relief and to share with her my exasperation at being made to wait, but instead, I blinked back the tears and whispered, "I know."

"Are you the mother?" a nurse asked, poking her head in the room.

"Yes," my mother replied as the nurse stepped in the waiting room trailed by a very tall doctor. The doctor exuded confidence and superiority, or perhaps I only perceived him that way from my youthful perspective. His blue eyes searched my face as if the answer to my problem was written somewhere on it.

Then came the disappointment. Instead of the instant relief I craved, there were unending questions, face probing, discussions, X-rays, and blood tests. At last, we were back in Dr. Garrett's office, but the thorough examination convinced me that there were complications to my case. Accompanied by two local doctors, Dr. Garrett informed us of what we could expect from treatment. He recommended a series of operations to remove the "growth of tissue" because he felt one surgery would not correct the problem for an eight-year-old. Nothing specific was revealed, not even a definite promise of freedom from my affliction.

"Is that all you can tell us?" my mom asked.

"I'm afraid that's all we can tell you for now," replied the doctor. I wanted to take my mom by the hand and flee from his presence. I wanted to tell him he did not know what he was talking about.

To think that we prayed so long and walked so far just to hear this lie … You must not know God, I thought angrily. *If you did, He would have told you exactly how to fix my face.*

I would never have openly resisted Dr. Garrett's prognosis, but silently I raged. In spite of my disapproval, my mom signed the necessary documents authorizing my first surgery. The date was scheduled for me to be admitted to the hospital. The activity surrounding me only increased my apprehension. In my perception, people went to the hospital to die.

Ordinarily, a trip to Castries meant new clothes or shoes for church or school. Sometimes, it meant a new, baldheaded doll or other toy at Christmas time. Whenever the trip occurred, all the siblings at home would receive their own treat, too. The children participating in the trip joyously returned home, eager to open a "goodie" bag from town that contained a treat for every brother and sister who was left behind. The anticipated excitement made the bus ride home seem unending. Nevertheless, the bus ride home from the doctor was surprisingly short that day.

As we stepped off the bus and started down the narrow, winding path, it was as if every step I took was one step away from my most cherished fantasy. Curious, peering eyes had always haunted my thoughts, so I created an image of myself in which my face was so well-reconstructed that I no longer was embarrassed by it. No longer would I hear, "That's too bad, Mrs. Rudolph. She was going to be your prettiest girl," concluding a battery of questions about my mysterious face.

This day I was supposed to return from Castries with the face I had imagined so I would be stared at for my beauty instead of my shame. Instead, I was helplessly disappointed, and yet I still felt the need to hide my true emotions behind another mask of indifference.

Faking my emotions became painful in the days that followed. I felt that everyone could see right through me. I wanted to die, but some strange power from within compelled me to continue living in my make-believe world for everyone else's sake.

I could have identified many reasons for severing my relationship with God. After all, Mom said God would take care of me, but He did not do it as I asked. Instead, I realized that if I ever needed the Lord, I surely needed Him now. Even in my despair, or perhaps because of it, I could not fathom life without God. I had come to rely upon the peace and assurance I experienced after spending time alone in prayer. Sometimes, during those moments, I simply cried—words were not necessary. It was then, in the silence of it all, that I felt His presence, and I knew that all would be well.

In His presence, I knew no shame or embarrassment. I knew He understood my desire to camouflage my pain and disappointment from others under a cloak of strength. He knew I was afraid that one weak moment would expose me to loved ones and give them the opportunity to discover the real me that I kept well hidden. I could imagine Him looking down from heaven understandingly. I could feel His arms cradling me for comfort. I longed to stay in that quiet place with Him forever. I knew that I simply needed to keep trusting and hoping. This would not be the end of my life.

After my private reflections, I had the courage to dry my tears and return to the real world. I drew on His strength to face the uncertainty of my admission to the hospital.

Chapter 2

———

My New Home

My hospital stay required my mom to make many difficult trips from our home to the city. She looked increasingly uncomfortable with her heavily pregnant stomach. When the day of my discharge finally came, it was a relief to me; I was grateful for both her sake and mine. I waited for my mom's arrival with my suitcases packed, so I would not have to stay one minute longer than necessary.

Occasionally, while I waited, my thoughts were interrupted by a friend's goodbye. Even the nurses stopped in to tell me they were glad I was going home, but they would miss me. This seemed a little odd to me: a child might miss a playmate, but why would the nurse miss me? If anything, they should be happy I was leaving, since the hospital was filled with more people than they could handle.

When my mom arrived, I remember one nurse saying, "Your daughter never complains and is so full of courage." That made me feel good inside because it showed me I had concealed my fears well.

It was impossible to tell if the procedure had been successful through all the swelling. I was leaving the hospital more disfigured than I had been when I arrived. However, the doctors assured my mom that the positive results would be obvious once my new injuries healed.

Numerous relatives from all over the island visited me while I recovered at home. I reveled in the extra attention I was receiving. My favorite aunt, Ruth, arrived and convinced my parents to allow me to live with her.

"It is not good to have her walk this long distance in the blistering sun to school," Aunt Ruth said. "That will surely harm her face when it is like this. In our parish, the school is only a short walking distance. Plus it is a very good school. Her education would be improved there, and she'll like it. My dear little Tina could use a younger sister for company."

Since the medical advice my parents received had included a warning to avoid extreme sun to my face, Aunt Ruth's argument made sense.

I was eager to go with Aunt Ruth. She had always been my role model. Her perseverance, uprightness, and helpfulness were known to all. When she convinced my parents to release me to her temporary custody, I felt very privileged. Even the thought of living with Tina, Aunt Ruth's only daughter, was thrilling. I longed to play with a big baby doll she owned.

As soon as I had completely recuperated from surgery, I was able to begin the country walk to my aunt's home with my brother. Once the excitement of the goodbyes were over, I found that I needed to walk very quickly in order to keep up with my brother, who was extremely tall and long-legged despite being only two years my senior. It was not long before the scorching noonday sun robbed me of my energy, and I began to fall behind.

"Come on," Joe encouraged me periodically.

Each time my steps would quicken but I could only maintain the pace for a short period of time.

"Are you tired?" He asked teasingly after a while.

"Uh, uh," I replied, shaking my head. I refused to let him see my weakness.

Again, I tried to walk faster. I began to worry if I did not keep up that he would say, "This is too much for you. Let's go back home." However, despite my resolve, I began to drag again.

"See, you are tired," he teased. "There's a store up the road where we can get some mopsy and rest for a while."

"Did you say 'mopsy'?" My mouth began to water at his mention of the favorite cookie.

"Yes, I said, 'mopsy.' You want to hear it again?" he joked.

That suggestion was enough to quicken my steps temporarily until we reached the store.

Even with the short break, the rest of the journey was so unbelievably exhausting that it became increasingly difficult to hide my fatigue.

"How far are we from Aunt Ruth's?" I asked repeatedly.

"Not too far," was the only reply he ever offered me.

"You're not lying, are you?" I asked.

"You want to pick some fat pokes?" Joe asked, ignoring my question.

"No!" I snapped. Normally, I would have been distracted again from the offer of my favorite wild fruit, but the walk was wearing on me.

"I thought you liked them."

"I don't want any today. I'm too tired," I replied, no longer trying to hide it.

We arrived at our destination shortly before dark. Exhausted from the journey, mixed emotions bubbled up inside me over the entire ordeal. I began to question if I belonged with my aunt at all. After supper, she wisely suggested that I retire for the night. I gave her no arguments, and drifted quickly to sleep.

After sleeping for a long time, I awoke late in the morning to a dilemma. After coming from a bustling house filled with eight children, this home appeared completely deserted. Tina was there, but my brother had already left on the long walk home and my aunt and uncle had left in the early hours to work on their farm.

"Where is my brother?" I asked.

"He's gone," replied Tina.

"Gone?" I bellowed. The weariness I felt from the day before had not worn off yet. To awake in a strange place without anything familiar threw me into near panic. A sudden and unfamiliar loneliness permeated my entire being. I had never felt so abandoned. Teardrops rolled down my face, and not once did I think of trying to hide my feelings. Tina did not try to hide that she was annoyed by my display, either.

For the first time, I realized that the joy of my life stemmed from my family. I was used to being surround by people. Even when I stayed in the hospital, there were people and activity around me. The only time life had been silent was during my time alone with God. Up to this point in my life, I was very unfamiliar with physical aloneness. The words "leave me alone" were meaningless in my home. At my aunt's house, I was alone without asking for it.

"Why didn't he wake me up?" I wondered aloud.

"'Cause Mama asked him not to." Tina was unaffected by my emotional outburst. She was four years older than me, and made no attempt to soothe my aching heart.

I sobbed continuously for hours. Irrationality came over me and I began to repeat, "My brother left me. Now I have nobody."

I did not know it at the time, but this experience prepared me for future separations from my family that I would soon experience. I thought the presence of one brother could have changed the situation, but it would have offered only brief comfort.

The adage "time is a great healer" proved factual. I got used to the loneliness of my new home, and I became excited about the first day of school. When the time finally came, there were typical questions I did not want to answer from other students.

"What's wrong with your face?"

"I don't know," was always my first response.

I never replied honestly that I did not want to talk about it. Still, denying knowledge of my condition allowed me to change the subject. Some of the students were very friendly and asked many questions about my home and the reason for my move here. They also vied to sit next to me in class. One girl, whose father owned a store, brought me lollipops bigger than the widest mouth.

Although I had adjusted to the newness of my aunt's home, the reality of living with her slowly set in. The traits I once respected in Aunt Ruth from a distance appeared to be brutal tyranny up close. At times she even seemed to be intolerant of any child, and it frightened me.

> I did not know it at the time, but this experience prepared me for future separations from my family that I would soon experience.

Her lists of rules were long and offered no room for error. Obedience was required.

Even washing dishes came with a long list of rules. If I forgot to put the soap in the right place or accidentally left it in the water, I would soon find my ear firmly captured between my aunt's thumb and forefinger. My aunt would lead me to the offending bar without releasing her grip regardless of the distance, and I would be expected to dry the soap, if necessary, and to return it to its proper location. I sympathized with Tina from the beginning. She never was spared a vicious beating for disobedience.

When I first received only warnings for my infractions, I began to believe that my aunt did not have the parental authority to punish me because I was not her child. She voluntarily made me a part of her family based on her concern for my well-being, and I was still a sick child in need of care and protection. These factors all made me feel exempt from her brutal punishments.

However, time soon proved me wrong. In fact, she had no respect for Tina or me. The physical, mental, and emotional abuse I had watched her exact on Tina did not take long to pour onto me, as well.

From childhood, I had a preoccupied mind that led me to be extremely forgetful. Long lists of detailed rules were not in my favor. I became more vulnerable to Aunt Ruth's abuses than her own daughter had been. I frequently forgot to meet her trivial requirements.

There were also many rules governing school items. School bags had a proper order (large items on the bottom and smaller ones on top) and needed to be properly stocked with our assigned items. At the end of the school week and usually after supper on Fridays, we presented our school bags to Aunt Ruth. Each bag was carefully inspected. If the bags were disorganized, we received some minor form of corporal punishment. If we were missing an item, the beating would be severe. I could never understand why she was so concerned about any of my missing items—my parents provided the money for my school supplies.

Keeping my bag organized according to my aunt's rules was an easy task but keeping track of all my supplies was not. Pens, pencils, paintbrushes, or colored pencils would often turn up missing regardless of how well I tried to keep track of them. I attributed my problems to art. I enjoyed both drawing and painting. Craving the praise teachers would bestow on my artwork and using art itself to escape from my daily life, I would frequently get lost in my work during that period. Too often, at the close of that period, I discovered a missing pencil, colored pencil, or paintbrush, which was never recovered. I began to suspect that a classmate would wander over to my desk in the guise of admiring my work and then steal something. Needless to say, missing items caused me much anxiety throughout the remainder of the week. I prayed and hoped that the culprit would return my possession before the coming Friday, but it never happened.

Chapter 3

Conflict

The long awaited school breaks provided some relief from my aunt's unhappy home, and I could look forward to spending the time with my biological family. The thought of roaming the countryside, picking wild fruits, and playing marbles with my paternal cousin or jumping ropes with my siblings was gratifying.

On these visits, I frequently felt the urge to speak to my mother about the discomforts of my new home. Inside, I was continually conflicted. On one hand, there was my aunt's cruelty, from which I longed to escape. On the other, I enjoyed the positive status of distinction I gained at my new school. In addition to my new friends, the school principal, "Sir (Mr. Bartholomew Gaspard)," showed significant confidence in me by frequently assigning me challenging responsibilities. I appreciated feeling useful. I considered the abuse at home a small price to pay in exchange for the feelings of gratuity and fulfillment at school. So, I kept silent.

I still had to make trips back to the hospital for additional surgery on my face. After one of my absences from school, Sir invited me to visit with his family. He informed me of doctors in the United States that could use more advanced procedures to deal with my blemish.

"Such treatments are very technical," he said.

I listened attentively while he described methods that involved plastic surgery. At the time, it sounded like a magical cure. Looking back, I wonder if any mention of a treatment was impressive.

My new goal became to find a way to the United States, so I could have access to this instant sounding cure. My prayer time had fallen off since moving in with my aunt. Although I was more alone than ever, the house never felt safe enough to go to God. My focus began to shift to what I could do using my own strength.

I knew I needed a good plan to leave the country. My family was not destitute. We had enough to survive, but there was not enough extra money to finance an expensive trip on one person's behalf. The sacraments of infant baptism, Holy Communion, and Holy Confirmation were annual expenses that had to be paid. In addition, we had many deceased loved ones who needed sufficient monetary offerings to the church, prayers, and candle lightings to assist them on their way from purgatory to heaven. Then there were the bus fares for the family to attend worship at the distant church on Sunday each week. With the welfare of every family member living and dead at stake, I could not even ask my family to dip into their already tight budget. My plan was more practical: work hard to finish school early, secure a good job, and save toward my trip to the United States. Finishing school quickly would also resolve the problems I was having in my aunt's home.

Making plans and putting them into action are two different things, of course. My home life with Aunt Ruth may have spurred me to finish school fast, but the abuse was certainly not helpful. Once set, it was obvious that the goal I had chosen was quite challenging from the start. I became resistant and resilient, forcing myself to attend school even after severe beatings. My mind became even more distracted as it focused on thoughts of pending beatings. However, my resolve hardened around my goal.

All my concentration was directed toward school. As a result, my grades escalated. As my grades went up, I was able to skip classes. This gave me the advantage of skipping grades. In St. Lucia at the time, sixth grade was the highest level of high school. At the age of thirteen, I entered sixth grade a year ahead of my peers. I was elated not only because I had advanced an entire grade, but also because I was a year from completing high school and the first phase of my dream goal.

However, at my aunt's home I had become stoical. The situation had driven me to lie in an effort to avoid beatings, even though it was never effective. Worse was that being caught in a lie meant twice the punishment and embarrassment. My character had been negatively impacted by the terror I suffered.

"I didn't see your pen," Aunt Ruth said after checking my bag.

"It was in the bag," I quickly replied.

Lying had become almost automatic by this time. I knew I would get caught, but a delay of a day or two would be better in my eyes.

"Here!" my aunt yelled, throwing the bag at me. "Find me your pen."

Of course, I knew the pen was no longer in the bag. I had lost it earlier in the week and had searched for it, continuously, to no avail since then. Afraid and desperate, I peered into the bag hoping against hope that it would be there as a result of some miracle. Suddenly, a thought entered my mind that seemed brilliant.

"Oh boy!" I hoped I sounded convincing enough. "Sir borrowed my pen and forgot to give it back."

Today was Friday. If I could convince my aunt I was telling the truth, she would ask me to bring it home Monday. I could devote the weekend to prayer and then maybe God would find the pen for me on Monday when I returned to school. Unfortunately, my idea did not work out as planned.

> I could not believe she would prove me a liar in front of Sir.

"Alright," responded Aunt Ruth. "I shall meet you after school on Monday, and I will ask your Sir about your pen."

I could not believe she would prove me a liar in front of Sir. He had been so good to me. I wavered momentarily and thought about just taking the cruel beating, but the damage had been done.

Against my will, I proceeded to school on Monday. The weekend had been the shortest and most miserable I ever experienced. Every spare moment between classes and during recess I searched for it. I asked everyone if he or she had my blue Atlas Fountain Pen. The end of the school day did not bring an end to my suffering. I was in anguish and praying that my aunt would forget to meet me as she had promised. Although I had not found my pen, I hoped that my prayers were answered differently. Exiting the school gate, I surveyed the area and was happy to see that my aunt was not waiting for me.

I joined a group of children who were happily chitchatting. I began to relax and decided that maybe I had dreamed Aunt Ruth's declaration. Then I recognized the familiar figure walking toward me. At her silent command, I turned around and walked with her toward the school. It did not take my aunt long to speak with Sir and confirm the lie I told. Sir's disappointment was evident. What followed was one of the most embarrassing moments of my life. My aunt proceeded to flog me right on the spot. Having spoken with Sir and found my pen-story untrue, she thought nothing of beating me right on the scene.

Although the shame of that moment remained with me most of my life, I continued to pursue my goal. The school year of 1966 slowly came to a close. Together with the other students, I looked ahead to the final exam for our high school diploma, or school certificate as we called it. Most of the other students were one year my senior, which gave me the ability to retake the test if I failed the first time. Still, I was filled with anxiety. My diploma was the pass to get out of my aunt's home, to secure my first job, and to begin the second phase of my future plan.

When the big day finally arrived, we waited impatiently together for the bus. Each of us was thoroughly prepared and was the top in our grade. We were all expected to succeed. We would not have been chosen to take the exam had it been otherwise because our school, The Babonneau Combined, maintained a reputation for effectively trained students. Our education had been carefully administered to ascertain the success of every student.

The bus took us to the educational building in Castries. The exam covered several subjects and failure to obtain a passing grade in any one of them disqualified students for the diploma unless, like me, they were being tested prior to their fifteenth birthday. I had an opportunity to retest on the failed subject, redeem the required grade in the subject, and acquire my diploma. Had I not desperately wanted to leave my aunt and begin Phase II, I would not have felt such urgency. I did not believe I could go through another year's extensive study under the critical eye of my aunt. To help me pass, I breathed a silent prayer, "Lord, please help me … especially with my arithmetic."

The hours passed by, long and tedious. But then it was time for the test covering arithmetic. I had never scored high in the subject, but I always seemed to pass in one way or another. As always, I had difficulty with the problem solving aspects, and this exam was no exception. The sound of the bell indicating my time was up occurred a little more than halfway through the complex problems. The tears threatened to fall, but I did my best to hide them while I handed the papers to the proctor.

I longed for immediate disclosure of the results. Although I had little hope of passing since I had not completed the arithmetic portion of it, I did not relish the thought of returning home for the vacation to wonder. After all, there was always the possibility of a miracle.

Dreadful thoughts plagued me throughout the time I spent at home with my immediate family. The consequence for me if I failed meant another year of agony with my aunt. My summer was depressing and restless, but the day we returned to school was no better. While those around me were able to engage in the usual chatter, I found myself wishing for quiet so I could spend the last moments hoping and praying for positive news. Sitting in class, a sudden hush came over the room as the distinctive footsteps approached in the hallway. The footsteps were rapid, and something about the clicking of the well-polished, hard sole, leather shoes reminded us of the stinging leather strap he carried in his left hand. This strap, which we named "The Police," demanded our utmost attention and best behavior. No one walked like our Sir.

There was an air of satisfaction about him as he stood before us.

Just tell me, I thought. *Did I pass, or did I fail?*

"It was a very good exam. The result is excellent." Relief spread through me when he said this, only to die as soon as he continued. "Only two insufficiencies," the next words from his mouth felt like a death sentence on my ears. I knew that I was one of them.

With a throbbing heart, I sat and listened to the names being called. It seemed like I waited forever. Then, there was a pause. I looked around because I thought I was the only one whose name had not been called, but I noticed that the most brilliant girl in the class, Stephanie, also did not have her results.

How can this be? I wondered as he called our names. But instead of handing us our papers, he asked us to accompany him to his office.

"It's quite a coincidence," he marveled, when we entered the room. After handing us our papers, he continued, "You both did remarkably well in all areas except arithmetic."

He continued to question us about the areas of our struggles and vowed to give us the utmost support so we would pass the following year.

"The good thing about this," he added, "is the fact that you both have one more chance."

I wanted to plead with him and beg him not to talk about next year. I was not sure I would be able to remain alive that long. As I looked down at my score, I thought about the cruelty of it all. I paid no attention to my A's or B's; my arithmetic score stood out boldly. It was only two points less than a passing C. It did not seem fair that I could come so close only to be disappointed.

Chapter 4

Out of the Frying Pan and Into the Fire

At this point, I should have returned home to my biological family and continued my education at the local school. Instead, I focused on the setbacks that could happen if my current curriculum was interrupted. The school at home was far inferior to the school near my aunt's house. At the Babonneau Combined, Sir and my teachers knew my strengths and knew what I needed to learn to pass the exam. I convinced myself that I had already established a good relationship with these teachers. They pushed me until "my good was better and my better best." Although their attitude was annoying at times, I now saw it as something useful that would help me to prevail in my goals. Somehow, I had come to believe that the only way to achieve tomorrow's joys and accomplishments was by completing my schooling here. True, my body bore scars from Aunt Ruth's wicked beatings, but I had survived these for almost six years. What was another year?

Despite my resolve, one night, I could not bear it any longer. Tina was the object of her mother's wrath that evening because of something to do with the relationship she had with her boyfriend. I listened attentively to the lecture behind the closed door. The sounds that followed were heart rending. I heard the dull thwack of a stick hitting Tina's plump flesh intermitted with unfamiliar banging and smacking sounds. I prayed that the God of heaven would rescue Tina even though she had only been unkind to me. Later, Tina informed me that her mother had kicked her, punched her, and slammed her head against the naked posts of the wood-framed house.

Finally, she was marched outside where a container of already prepared salt water was waiting. Aunt Ruth poured it over all Tina's fresh wounds to enhance the pain of the torture. When Tina revealed the atrocities that had been done to her, my decision to tolerate Aunt Ruth for another year was changed. There was no way I would allow my aunt to torment me any longer. I had been pushed many times while living under her roof, but I knew I could contain my temper only so far. As the tortures grew worse, it was only a matter of time before I would turn on my aunt.

Before I could come up with a good strategy, I became involved in something that was sure to earn severe punishment once discovered. I decided that I was going to pack a small bag and take the bus home at the first opportunity. The rest of my items would keep until I could return to retrieve them. My primary focus was to get out while everyone was still breathing.

However, a few days passed and I had still not been able to leave. Again, I wavered on my resolve to return home. Aunt Jane was another nearby relative. If I moved to her house, I could still stay in the school that had become precious to me. I knew her husband, Mr. Bert, was a drunkard, but I would only be living with him—not married to him. Aunt Jane did not approve of Aunt Ruth's cruel discipline. I knew she would be a sympathetic ear to my cause. I saw this as the perfect solution to all my troubles.

That very same day, at dusk, I walked the short cut to Aunt Jane's house, hurrying to reach my destination before dark. Once I entered the house, I poured out my story of woe and was welcomed into my vision of a more humane household.

Again, I focused on the first facet of my plan, but it only took a few days to discover that the household where I now resided was equally as turbulent. Mr. Bert was not a good provider because of his alcoholism. This meant that there was never enough income to provide fresh, nutritional meals and other essentials. My parents sent me a weekly allowance of food, but often the family of five used it to feed all of us. I found myself frequently going to school hungry. Thankfully, my friends were very kind and would always share their lunches. I also quickly learned to save pennies and dimes for nutritional treats instead of candies and chewing gum.

One of the worst things about living with Aunt Jane was that it became my responsibility to go to the rum shop several times a week to purchase Mr. Bert's liquor. Although he went to the rum shop after mass on Sundays for a treat, he preferred to drink his liquor at home the rest of the week. I was not married to him, but I still had to run errands for him.

I hated carrying Mr. Bert's bottle home in the telltale brown paper sack. I had developed a crush on a boy named Tommy, and the entire time I worried that he or one of my peers would see me. Tommy was my best friend's brother and constantly asked about me, so I imagined he was my sweetheart. In my mind, I had already written our love story: I would return from the United States, my deformities gone and my goals achieved. Tommy would ask me to marry him and we would live happily ever after. I would have been mortified if this dream man had witnessed me supporting my uncle's habit. I tried to go to the store as close to nightfall as possible when most of the people my age were out of sight.

One night as I was walking home from this distasteful task under the half-lit sky, a distant relative from a prestigious family joined me. As if sensing my fears, he promised to walk me home. Although uninvited, my companion seemed harmless enough and I was thankful for the company.

We made small talk, but as the path went past a little shed, I found myself shoved into it by his overwhelming strength. I was overwhelmed by the smell of bananas, which were stored in the shed until shipment to the main town could be arranged.

"What are you doing?" I asked softly, trying not to draw outside attention out of fear I would be shunned. All the while I tried to free myself from his strong hold.

"This won't take long," he replied calmly, as if we were having a normal conversation.

"No, Sam! No!" I pleaded quietly, careful to keep my voice low.

I feared the publicity that could result from involving a third party. Being different because of natural causes was enough; I was not about to become a "bad girl" and bear another mark of negative distinction.

Unable to summon help from the outside because of my fear of shame, my perpetrator soon defeated my matchless resistance. Helplessly pinned to the ground and still whispering, "No, Sam! No!"

I experienced one of my bitterest moments of pain and anguish. It happened so fast and unexpectedly that the brown paper sack housing the bottle of rum was still clinched in my hand when my attacker released me and drifted back into the night.

Somehow, I found the courage to pull myself together and continued the walk to my aunt's home alone. On the way, I came to the decision that no one would know my shame. I blamed myself, in part, for this wicked encounter. I determined not to expose myself to more humiliation by revealing this encounter. Ignorant of what I had lost, I thought I would conceal it for life.

> Being different because of natural causes was enough; I was not about to become a "bad girl" and bear another mark of negative distinction.

Although I was alone and frightened, I dealt with the immediate and long-term effects that resulted. Again, I drowned myself in my obsession to finish school and change my place of residence. I had been unable to run from Aunt Ruth's house to a new, better home, but I still believed I would be able to manage my own way. Once I had finished my school and begun the next phase of my plan, I would no longer need to fear unwanted chaperones following me home from the liquor store.

Unfortunately, the plan I had laid out for myself was interrupted again a little over a week later. This time, I was alone at home when Mr. Bert arrived from work. He walked into the room with an unfamiliar, malicious grin on his face and advanced toward me.

"What do you want?" I asked as I took a step back from him in dismay.

Ignoring my question, he plunged at me as if he was a wild beast and groped me with his hands. My frustration at being a victim again so soon after the first incident overcame me and a sudden strength filled my being. I shoved him with tremendous force and he stumbled backward. After a few steps, he was able to regain his balance but stared at me wickedly while catching his breath. In the moment, I decided his abuse of alcohol had robbed him of physical strength. Later, I came to realize my advantage over him truly came from providential intervention.

"I'll be sure to tell my aunt about this!" I exclaimed, bluffing.

To tell Aunt Jane would be foolish; I did not dare disrespect her like that. Sex was a dirty word, and even if I could find the true courage to say it, I didn't think my aunt would believe me. She loved her husband and was his chief enabler.

Thankfully, my bluff paid off momentarily, and he left me alone. Early the next morning, long before it was time to awake for school, he came into my room.

"Wake up," he said tapping me on the shoulder. "I left you fifty cents on the table to pay your bus fare home. You can't stay here any longer."

I did not want to believe what he was telling me. My goal was to finish school here. If he was kicking me out of his house, I had no other options that would allow me to do that. Unable to accept reality, I told myself I was dreaming.

Some time after he left, I finally forced myself out of bed and walked toward the kitchen table. Sure enough, there was fifty cents. My uncle must have wanted me out of his house before I had a chance to relate his indecency to my aunt.

Staring at the money that marked the end of my goal to receive a diploma from this school, I thought, *You can keep your money. I'll find my way home.*

I had few things, so planning my departure didn't take long. Dressed in my school uniform, I headed into the early morning country air. It was refreshing against my face despite feeling that my dreams were crumbling. By noon, the blazing sun found me scuffling along an almost abandoned path. My discomfort finally matched my feelings; I was truly alone, without a sibling to guide me.

Weak from being deprived of basic nutrients, feeling utterly forsaken and lost, I remembered the relationship I once had with the Lord. I recalled the time when I was never too busy to listen to His soft, beckoning voice encouraging or instructing me. I remembered my childlike faith in God and how I had trusted Him with all my doubts and fears. I began to see my trip home, filled with internal and external struggles, as a reminder that I did not have to do it all myself.

Somehow, in my quest for success, I had exchanged the personal relationship I once had with the Lord for a self-reliant attitude. In my mind, I had convinced myself that God wanted me to take hold of my life. Who was I to be constantly imposing on His time? To sob on His shoulder and talk to him about every little thing in my life was presumptuous. I saw the few successes I had in school and with my friends as proof that I could excel and reach for the stars without relying on the strength of the Lord.

Yes, I had continued attending church and singing in the choir as a matter of routine, but my secret time in earnest prayer became unnecessary to me through the years in my aunts' homes. On the road that day, I realized that I had been beating my head against a wall and exposing myself to unnecessary pain and suffering because I believed it was in my power to direct the course of my life. When presented with a situation, instead of handing it over to the Lord, I was determined to bend and tailor it into my mold to meet my desires.

I realized that I had utterly failed in my solo efforts. As I neared the end of the day's journey, I wiped my weeping eyes and made this solemn vow: "Lord, if You will take me back and give me another chance, I will come to You with all my plans."

That one promise seemed to lighten my load and lift the shadows from the path I traveled. Weary steps sprung forward with hope. I was almost home, where I would receive the love of my family; but most importantly, I was home in the arms of a loving God. I can express the feeling no better than it is expressed in the words of the following song:

Weighed with grief and burdened
dreams, a wounded heart for mercy
screams. I hear Him say, "I'm very
near; give me your doubts, your hurt
and fear...."

Oh, wondrous love that beckons me
Look beyond my turbulent sea.
None other can lead me home
like gentle hands beyond the dome.

—Author unknown

Chapter 5

Behind Every Cloud, a Silver Lining

I soon found that my new life of commitment and trust in the Lord presented a continuous challenge. I later discovered the apostle Paul stated it best when he said, "For I know that nothing good dwells in me, that is, in my flesh; for the willing is present in me, but the doing of the good is not. For the good that I want, I do not do, but I practice the very evil that I do not want. But if I am doing the very thing I do not want, I am no longer the one doing it, but sin which dwells in me" (Rom. 7:18–20).

Still, after years following my own path, I was determined to follow the path set out by God. After all, everything I had done on my own had ended undesirably. I now knew that it was imperative to follow God's plans.

At first, I believed it would be easier to surrender to God's will if I had a passive nature. Then I thought, *What if I never heard the voice of my inner sinful self?* That way I would only be able to listen to God's voice. I prayed fervently for the Lord to silence my sinful self, but it was to no avail. Looking back with improved understanding of the gift of free will, I know why God never answered this prayer. Although God wishes to lead and instruct us in every aspect of our lives, He is not desirous to force our hand in matters. The Creator knows what is best for his children. If He forced us to do His will, we would be nothing more than animated dolls in his hands.

> I prayed fervently for the Lord to silence my sinful self, but it was to no avail.

In my case, I was still not willing to give over complete control of my plans to the Lord. Since I had not gained extensive knowledge of God's Word, the only medium I could find to test whether it was God's Will was to pursue my will and wait for God to open or shut the door on it. If a result was still negative after pursuing a goal, I would understand that God did not approve; He was shutting the door. On the other hand, if the results were positive, the outcome would reveal God's approval. Had I thought about it, perhaps I would have recognized the similarity to the way I did things at my aunts' homes. After pursuing my own plan for my life, it ended in pain and therefore I retreated.

It was not until I experienced my new birth that I began to understand how to walk by faith and not by sight. After studying the scriptures, I learned to follow the leading of the Holy Spirit. By understanding the sanctification process, I realized that my thinking before had been clearly flawed. While doing right and living a moral life in our human strength can have some worthwhile repercussions, the process may be filled with unnecessary pain and regret. In the end, it can cause more damage despite the high ideals behind it. On the other hand, total surrender to His will may result in discomfort and disappointments along the way, but the end product is always good for everyone involved. Before my new-birth experience, my concept of doing right deviated from that of true godliness. I simply needed to surrender to the Holy Spirit.

As I applied the new concept of closed and open doors to my life, I reassessed my life plan. I knew I had done everything humanly possible to acquire a high school certificate, but it had ended in disappointment. My simplistic deduction convinced me that obtaining a certificate was not necessary to access God's will for my life.

After two surgeries on my face at the St. Lucia hospital, I ended up with terrible disfigurement that seemed worse than the initial mark. Nothing my parents or the doctors said could convince me of the necessity for a third surgery.

I was certain my help would come in the United States. That had been my plan from the first. I had struggled to complete Phase I, so I decided it was time to move to Phase II. I resolved to find a job and save enough money to facilitate my ultimate dream: medical assistance in the United States. Once the money was saved in a quick and efficient manner, I could pursue Phase III to receive the miracle surgery. After reuniting with my biological family, I started job searching without a school certificate.

The process was full of challenges and disappointments. No one needed the services I offered. Many said they had no vacancies or that I was just too young.

In St. Lucia, several decades ago, gainful employment was limited to the educated, adult population. Consequently, my quest for employment at fourteen years old without a high school diploma was unusual.

I concluded that employment had been a door shut by God, but at the same time, I could not understand why. I was dismayed, confused, and at the point of returning home. *Surely*, I thought, *God must have a more appropriate plan for me.* Unwilling to give up on Phase II, I questioned whether I had exercised all human power to find a job. Suddenly a new idea began to form in my mind.

Mr. Livingston was the prime minister at the time, and I knew he was influential enough to get me a job on recommendation. I was from the Bardinee—the population responsible for a large number of his votes. In addition, my parents had high regard for him, and my mom made occasional visits to his office. She said he was a good man. Perhaps it was time for me to test that opinion.

Although it was late, I hurried along, unable to refrain myself from pursuing my new lead. Inside, I feared that I might not be able to see him because of the lateness of the day, but now that I had my idea, I did not want to turn back from it.

Immediately, upon entering the office I rushed past the waiting area and approached the receptionist, who was occupied with her typewriter.

"Excuse me," I interrupted self-importantly. "Is Mr. Livingston in?"

"Do you have an appointment?" she asked, ignoring my question.

"No," I responded, quick to add, "but this is urgent."

"What is your name?" she inquired.

"Rita Polius, daughter of Mrs. Joanna Rudolph." The whole conversation began to make me feel somewhat insignificant, so I used my mother's name as a passport.

"Have a seat," she ordered, making her way to the entrance of Mr. Livington's office.

It occurred to me that I should have sat down with the others in the waiting area when I first arrived. *Well, it's too late now*, I argued with myself. *Besides, there was no sign saying I needed to do that.* Just then the door opened, and to my amazement, I was ushered in to visit with the prime minister.

Mr. Livingston listened as I unfolded my need for employment in order to facilitate my trip to the United States.

"Someone in this town should have something to offer you," he said after voicing his concern for my situation. "Let me place some calls."

Coincidentally, the last person who had interviewed me was the first person he called. Although, the man had initially refused to hire me, when I returned to him with a note from the prime minister, Mr. Jameson escorted me through the Dry Goods Whole Sale Department where I was scheduled to begin work the following Monday.

It was clear to me that God had opened this door so that I could embark on Phase II. My first job was a miracle! Joy flooded my soul. I could already picture myself moving on from Phase II to Phase III.

The first two weeks on the job was a gratifying experience. Eager to learn and succeed, I laid in bed many nights rehearsing my responsibilities. I resolved to work hard and advance because not only was this job a necessary tool to achieve my dreams—but I was determined to prove that a teenager could be just as effective as an adult.

Then my first payday arrived. I tore open the envelope with eagerness and excitement, but what a disappointment it turned out to be. Seventeen dollars and fifty cents for two weeks of hard labor not to mention the expenses that I had incurred during the time commuting and obtaining appropriate attire. My naïve plan had been to save half my paycheck toward Phase III. The reality of this paycheck was that I did not make enough to pay for even my current essentials.

At the end of the day, I returned home with a sad heart. I explained the situation to my mom and she advised me to pursue a job as a seamstress. A single-parent seamstress lived approximately two miles from my home and benefited regularly from my father's produce. She was a family friend and was within walking distance, so I could forego bus fare, and she would welcome me as an apprentice.

This was sound advice, considering that sewing was one of the highest paid jobs for women in those days. However, when I inquired about the position, I found that to be a qualified seamstress required at least two year's training without pay. Once I could earn an income, I knew it would probably take another two to three years before I could save the funds to accommodate Phase III. The continuous disfigurement of my face created urgency. I thanked her and turned the position down.

Lady, I just don't have five years to spare, I thought. *I'll probably be dead by then.* Aside from the pressure of time, I had never seen myself sewing during Phase II. My interests were mainly in human services, particularly those of a civil servant or social worker.

I was filled with apprehension but chose to continue my job. I fooled myself into believing that there had been some mistake and my next payday would rectify the problem. I felt completely baffled when the next and subsequent paydays found me holding checks that were no different. My Phase III dreams dissolved before my eyes.

The Bible defines faith as "the assurance of things hoped for, the conviction of things not seen" (Heb. 11:1). I did not have this faith, and I could not believe that the Lord would be able to provide. Instead of trusting, I thought of a plan to decrease my expenses, save more, and prepare myself for a better paying job. I persuaded my mom to discuss boarding arrangements with a friend of the family who lived within walking distance to my job.

The friend agreed that I could stay with her family rent-free. However, I was responsible for providing my food and household needs. I did not foresee any problems with that. I knew I could count on my parents' garden for fresh fruits and vegetables, and when necessary, I could help myself to some household supplies from Mom.

The other part of my plan also posed no hardship to me. Another friend of my family, Mr. Dikes, owned and taught a small secretarial school. A secretary's skills were in greater demand and therefore the position paid more. The monthly fee to learn basic typing was $10. Mr. Dikes, who was godfather to one of my sisters, agreed to only charge me $5 a month. I knew that secretarial positions required both typing and shorthand to obtain top pay. I was tempted to enroll for both courses, but even in the idealistic future I had imagined, I was constrained by my limited income. I settled for just typing classes.

As you might have expected, my plan was not as smooth in its execution as I thought it would be. Despite careful planning and budgeting, my money did not cover my needs. Expenses for food and household needs far exceeded the amount I had anticipated. The woman I lived with who owned the house was an abandoned housewife and the mother of three children. She already had difficulties providing for her family. Thus, the little I provided was not an addition but a necessity. When my commodities were depleted, I went without until I replaced them by sacrificing something else.

Consequently, the excess money I spent to survive through the month did not allow me enough extra to meet my other financial obligations. When I couldn't pay the $5 for typing lessons at the end of the month, the amount was carried forward; this happened more than once. The inconvenience resulted in undesirable absences from classes, sometimes for months. Initially, I planned a single year to raise the necessary funds to pursue Phase III. As each barrier began to rise in front of me, my one-year goal was significantly extended.

During these times when it seemed the clouds were constantly threatening my sky, I came close to surrendering in defeat. However, I was not completely faithless. My limited measure of faith gave me glimpses of the silver lining hiding behind the clouds. It was during those times when I felt compelled to keep up the good fight.

Chapter 6

Pride Versus Integrity

After two years of working for Mr. Jameson, I was still far from realizing my Phase II goal. However, my circumstances had improved greatly. My salary was raised from $17.50 to $35 biweekly. With my increase in pay, I had managed to save $105 toward my goal.

I had also changed my residence. I found a senior citizen named Tina to share a house with me. This arrangement had two advantages to my first boarding experience: I was sharing with one person instead of four people, and Tina's adult children lived in England and supported her financially. There were also disadvantages that I tried to overlook: Tina constantly used obscene language that I despised; and she had severe physical limitations. Part of the terms of my staying there meant that I was to do most of the housekeeping in exchange of free rent and improved nutrition.

Tina was a good cook. As long as I contributed to the groceries, she fed me well. Overall, this situation could have been a boost to achieving my life goal, but I still had two important lessons to learn.

Tina's home was a long distance from the bus route, so it was almost impossible for my mom to get there. A few private owners limited the public transportation system at the time, and it frequently caused commuter inconvenience. Mom could not miss her bus home, so after a long day selling produce in the central market, she would leave a basket of luscious fruits and vegetables with a friend. Mindful of the time, she would then rush through the stores to shop for necessary supplies. Sometimes, she even had a few minutes to walk up the flight of steps to the second floor of the large department store where I worked and ask me what I needed. She never failed to remind me of the basket and often gave me her pocket change that would amount to a few precious dollars. If she did not have time for personal contact, she would leave messages with my coworkers on the first floor.

Even though these people never failed to convey Mom's message reminding me to pick up the basket, I often ignored it. I suppose my mom thought I neglected it out of forgetfulness, but the truth was that my pride kept me away. Considering how tight my funds were, I should have welcomed news about a basket full of food just waiting for me. However, I was convinced that walking the streets with a basket of provisions in hand was "country" and unbecoming of me, the new town girl. When I neglected to pick up the basket, I had to pay Tina for her order of delivered produce.

On one hand, I was impatient to achieve my goals. I did not expect that God would drop the money in my lap for Phase III, but I had a very youthful belief that if I started working I would be earning more money than my experience and education offered. I grew impatient as my dreams stagnated and lost sight of my values. It even crossed my mind more than once that God loved everybody and cared for everybody except me. As a result, my personality changed for the worse. Without the assurance of God's love, I felt like an orphan. Ironically, I was pushing myself away from my country routes and probably helping to increase my feelings of abandonment again.

My sense of not belonging often resulted in losing some of my values in an effort to keep up appearances rather than accepting reality. In this frame of mind, prayer and meditation seemed insignificant. I began to pray out of habit, not necessity, once more. Meanwhile, the emptiness within me from pulling back in my personal relationship with the Lord constantly demanded a filler.

Determined to experience some level of satisfaction, I was easily persuaded to skip school in exchange for going to the movies with friends on our days off and I became very conscious of criticism. I wanted to be a people pleaser regardless of the negative impacts on my values. When my friends planned a shopping spree, I consented even though I could not afford it. When my friends disapproved that I went to the country on the weekends, I complied and stayed with them to enjoy the pleasures of the town even though I would have preferred spending the time with my family.

This change of lifestyle had a bitter price which included more financial problems. I continued to neglect the basket at the market and continued adding unnecessary costs to my life. Between paydays when I ran short of funds and could not pay the high prices at the market or pay Tina for her delivery orders, I was forced to abstain from nutritious meals. I often went to work after a breakfast of tea and crackers and repeated the same fare for lunch and supper. At first, my stomach complained, but I eventually became used to it. Soon it became habitual. After days of scarcity and starvation, I boarded the bus to my country home. There I would partake lavishly of home cooked meals and fresh fruits, hoping that would suffice for my days of deprivation.

Needless to say, the continuous deficiency of food resulted in involuntary weight loss which was not surprising. Then I began to get a skin rash and boils on parts of my body including my hands and neck. Tina had a wealth of home remedies for my condition. I tried each one, even applying hot banana peels, which actually made the situation worse.

When I realized I had become desperate enough to try something as ridiculous as that, I knew the situation had become critical. I made an appointment on my next payday to see one of the town's best doctors for the precious sum of $10. With no better alternatives and constant itching, I welcomed good medical advice at any cost.

I turned to prayers for a cost effective cure, and, thankfully, God answered them. The doctor gave me a prescription and told me to begin applying it immediately.

"Now, young lady," he continued. "Tell me about your eating."

"What do you mean?" I asked, trying to conceal my embarrassment and guilt.

Ignoring my question, he proceeded to inform me that my symptoms were the result of inadequate nutrition. He further instructed me to eat three balance meals a day,

A sense of deception and guilt pervaded my innermost soul, as I reflected on the circumstances resulting to that fate. Later on when I read, "A man's pride will bring him low, but a humble spirit will obtain honor" (Prov. 29:23), I was able to relate it to this point in my life.

During my teen years, the experience alerted me to the destructive effects of "pride." Through prayer, I sought deliverance from my vanity, but my constant habit of keeping God at arm's length left a void that was not filled until four years later when I experienced conversion.

Chapter 7

Playing With Fire

Although my fall from pride was hard, I had another lesson to learn at the age of eighteen. The Bible says, "Can a man take fire in his bosom and his clothes not be burned?" (Prov. 6:27). I was about to learn the truth of this verse.

My first supervisor assisted me to a new position at the third largest discount store in the city and that gave me a $10 biweekly pay increase. I was responsible for stocking, dispatching, and reporting depleted stock with a co-worker, James, who was six years my senior.

Before long, James and I were meeting outside of the work place. To me he seemed kind, caring, and impressive. During this time of emotional emptiness and raging hormones, I was vulnerable to him. I enjoyed his attention, and I was flattered by his affection, but I never imagined things going any further. I naïvely thought this would come later, after my return from the United States and our marriage.

He said many sweet things, like, "I love you… I want to be with you forever… I like this or that about you." At the time I did not realize these things were not the same as saying, "I will marry you… We will work hard to build a happy home… We will live happily ever after."

I thought we both enjoyed our relationship as it was, but I eventually gave in to the pressure to have sex with him. I thought that was the only way to prove my love for him. In my mind, I thought, *This one time will not hurt.* But it did.

In the subsequent days and weeks, I thought the situation was behind me. As the months went on, people began to make several comments about my increased weight. I brushed this off as complementary. I could always out eat my siblings, but I had been underweight. My recent bout with malnutrition also made me happy to be gaining weight. Then I began to hear what I perceived to be cruel lies about my pregnancy. I was late almost three months, but that was not unusual for me—I had missed my period several times in the past.

In addition, I had convinced myself that only women who were married got pregnant. It was true that I had been poorly educated in this area. This, in part, was because of my sheltered, ignorant life. My mom's only instructions to me on the subject were, "You are a big girl now, so be careful."

My peers were probably as naïve as I was. During school, we talked negatively about the one "Very bad girl" who dropped out of school because of her pregnancy. Even though I was now in the same situation, I kept denying it was true and refusing to accept reality.

The gossip about my pregnancy reached me through my favorite cousin.

"Smallie," she said, addressing me by my nickname, "My mom told me you are pregnant. She said auntie knows it and is waiting for you to tell her. Don't you know you are pregnant?"

Although she appeared to be genuinely concerned, I thought she was taking sides with the others, and I disliked her for it. However, she persisted. Since she was married with two children and more experienced with this subject than I was, I agreed to see a doctor.

After the examination, the doctor wrote me a prescription and told me I needed a follow-up appointment. He did not inform me of my pregnancy, and I was too scared to inquire about it. I perceived the prescription would solve the problem. *Surely, he would tell me if I were pregnant. That's why I paid him*, I thought.

At the next appointment, though, my worst nightmare came true. My pregnancy was confirmed, so I could no longer deny it. I exited the doctor's office with a prescription for prenatal vitamins and my doctor's instructions for a healthy pregnancy.

Internally and externally, my world had crashed. I may have been confronted with the undeniable reality of my situation, but I could not think of one good reason to justify the pregnancy. I believed I was a good girl. And then there were my many goals. They did not include accommodations for raising a child.

> I was left standing alone, drenched in my sorrow without my dreams, hopes, and aspirations.

I did not recognize my own failures. By the system of open or shut door that I had created and offered to God, I should have easily been able to see the connection between my willful behavior and the consequences that I perceived to be entirely negative. But I did not accept my sin for what it was.

Why did the Lord permit this? I wondered. *Is it not enough that I have to deal with my problem face? How unfair can you be, God?* These were my constant questions through the remaining six months of my pregnancy. It was easier to blame God than to acknowledge I had played with fire and gotten burned.

Accepting the responsibility for my ordeal would happen in the future, but the painful ramifications of it were instantaneous and progressive. For the first time in my life, I was enveloped in self-pity—I did not know how to face my parents, my siblings, my peers, my admirers, or the world. I was left standing alone, drenched in my sorrow without my dreams, hopes, and aspirations.

I walked unconsciously from the doctor's office to my workplace. I felt all eyes were searching me, filled with unasked questions. I had no answers for my immoral, stupid behavior. I walked toward James' work area haltingly. I knew I must tell him. I did not anticipate that he would react with an outburst of joy, but I knew that he at least would help me. He was, after all, a father-to-be.

To my relief, James was not in. He had left work early with a delivery and would not return until the next morning. It gave me more time to plan my approach.

That night, I lay awake through long hours of contemplation. I forced myself to acknowledge the recent changes in my relationship with James. I now saw that our personal contact, despite working together, had been diminished, and I was uncertain of who was responsible for the avoidance. We even avoided eye contact during work. I knew the reason for my change in attitude but had to wonder about his reason.

I greeted the morning with despair. Overwhelmed, tired, and sleep deprived, I tried to turn off my mind, but it did not work. I managed to enter the workplace early to prepare for my meeting with James. I wanted to talk with him before he left for the field. He must have known my reason for standing there awaiting his arrival. We both stood in silence until finally, with teary eyes and quivering lips, I stated regretfully, "You are going to be a father."

His silent response told all. I realized he was not thinking about love, romance, fatherhood, or a serious relationship with me. His look conveyed the message clearly – I was alone. His strange behavior in the days following justified my perception.

James' response added to my pain. However, I had two remaining anchors, my cousin, Bebet, and my supportive neighbor. I especially looked forward to lunch with my cousin on that cloudy day. For the first time, I audibly explained my life-plan, including all the disappointments I suffered from age thirteen in pursuit of it.

The result was rewarding. Bebet offered to take temporary custody of my infant shortly after birth so that I could pursue my goal and return the child to me upon my return from America. She also offered to assist me with my needs during prenatal care and childbirth. I was past the first trimester and had no clue of what was involved, but Bebet did. She assisted me in making a priority list, which included the savings I would need to build. I would have access to the accessories she obtained for her three babies, including clothing and a cradle. I was grateful beyond words.

Bebet's intervention helped me to gradually accept my situation. It also served to remind me of God's disapproval but not condemnation. He was extending a second chance to me. God also manifested His love through my wealthy neighbor friend. I appreciated her financial support, but her moral support was worth more than words can express.

These two women helped me to overcome my crushed emotions of self-pity and embarrassment and to resume my decisiveness and perseverance.

I also discovered that James was not the man I first imagined when I began seeing him outside of work. During our relationship, I did not think to inquire about any other girls he might be seeing, and he did not volunteer the information. I took it for granted that I was his only girl. He lived in my neighborhood, so when he was not with me I thought he was in the company of his male peers. On the nights when I walked home from secretarial school, I looked forward to James' abrupt exit from his peer group, under the streetlight on the corner, to escort the rest of my walk home.

However, shortly after informing James of my pregnancy, when the fragments of my life were finally mending without his help, there he was in our usual pause-before-saying goodnight place. On that night, I was not the girl standing with him, nor did he acknowledge me as I reluctantly walked past them. I realized my cherished hope that he would return to me was futile but seeing him with someone else was terrible. I later learned that James and the other girl had been together for years.

Chapter 8

A Strange Encounter

One day, my friend and neighbor, Loral, shared that my mom was in the hospital. Loral worked in the hospital and offered to walk there with me. A walk to the hospital when visiting a new mother or someone recovering from minor surgery, under the evening sky with sleeping stars and a full moon, could be very relaxing.

This situation was different; the patient was my mother. When I saw her three weeks before, she appeared fine. I wondered what could have happened in such a short time that would necessitate a hospital stay. I hoped whatever the problem was, it would be discovered quickly. However, a feeling of foreboding came over me. Although we hurried to get there, we arrived near the end of visiting hours. It seemed as if the journey took much longer than normal because of the fear I felt.

The woman in the hospital bed did not resemble my mother. She looked as if a ghost had visited her. Peering through sullen eyes that conveyed more than her words, she managed to whisper, "I'm alright. I just haven't been able to sleep or eat."

"Why?" It almost sounded like I was demanding an explanation from her for her physical deterioration.

"That's what the doctors are trying to find out," she replied. "They have taken a lot of different tests; it won't be long before they find the cause."

Though she tried to sound confident, Mom was not convincing.

As visiting hours came to a close, the nurse entered the room and gave my mom two pills that I assumed were sleeping agents. After informing her that the dosage had been increased, she asked "Are you going to sleep for us tonight?"

It was almost as if she was pleading with my mom. As the guard went down the hallway tingling the bell to announce the end of visiting hours, we hurried out, extremely concerned with my mom's lack of sleep and poor condition.

Because I was the only family member living within walking distance from the hospital, I added visitation with my mom, twice a day, to my priority list. After a week, the doctors were still unable to determine what was wrong with her. They finally concluded that the situation would resolve itself in time and discharged her from the hospital.

I was outraged. *What good is a hospital that discharges people without a cure? I hope we never have to set foot in this place again,* I thought.

As I predicted, my mom did not get better. Three weeks later my father returned her to the hospital because her declining health made it necessary.

My eldest sister, Martha, had normally been called upon to care for the family when Mom could not, usually because of the annual or biannual birth of a sibling. However, Martha had moved to Canada three years earlier. That made me the eldest sister in the family.

Until this point, though, I had been too preoccupied with my personal concerns to learn how to engage in physical giving. In fact, I had always been the recipient. All the good things I had planned to do to help my family were pushed into the future or at least until after I had resolved my own problems. During this time when I was learning about giving, the third eldest sister was more successful at taking Martha and Mom's place.

I then realized I needed to make plans to help my family immediately. I altered my schedule from visiting home once a month to commuting on a daily basis. This allowed me to witness first hand the source of my mom's sleeplessness.

Until I began spending nights at home, my father had withheld the source of Mom's trouble from me. I discovered her sleep deprivation was not related to an inability to fall sleep. Rather, she was awakened night after night by unseen hands gripping her throat. It was as if they were determined to choke her.

The first time I encountered this, I was speechless. Once I knew the source of her trouble, every unwelcome sound or movement in the rear bedroom drew me to Mom's bedside.

It was not unusual for me to toss and turn for hours longing for my own sleep to come. A weak groaning from my parents' bedroom would interrupt the stillness and gain intensity over intervals of quietude. Urged out of bed by fear that my mom would die, I rushed into the room where I could see my mother was engaged in a contest with an unseen force. When not panting for breath, she managed to whisper her prayers while clutching the cross pinned to her nightgown.

I would watch in horror as the battle raged for approximately 30 minutes. Then, with tears of relief streaming down her face, Mom would lay motionless. When her breathing returned to normal, she would let out a sigh of relief and say, "It's over now. Please pray with me."

The dawning of each day was a relief even though my days were tormented by thoughts of the night. During the day, Mom was weak from her nightly struggle. Every night seemed as if it could be her last night alive.

Throughout the ordeal, many friends, neighbors, and relatives visited to give their support. Whispers spread about the need to consult familiar spirits on Mom's behalf, but no one would have dared present the idea to Mom. She was a reputable, godly woman filled with strong faith. Her spiritual anchor was prayer.

One day, a concerned neighbor approached us with a variation on this idea. The neighbor had heard of a man, who used what he advertised as God-given power to heal people who were afflicted like my mom. Where most mediums were known to consort with the devil, this man stated that he only interacted divinely with the saints. He never did work for those wishing to cause harm to others.

Father was desperate to help Mom, so this information seemed to be his last chance for help. He happily brought the news to his wife, feeling there could finally be healing for her. She was very uncertain. Mom wanted to be free of her trouble, but she held to her beliefs.

"Who did you say he talks with?" Mom inquired cautiously.

"I was told that he is able to speak with the saints," replied my dad.

"OK," said Mom. "I'll give him a try. But I will not listen to him if I see any sign that he has dealings with the devil."

This seemed acceptable to all of us. Part of my family's religious belief taught us that it was normal and necessary to consort with those who are dead for help. We frequently asked dead saints to intercede on our behalf in church, so it opened us up to being deceived in this way.

Had we been raised to study the Bible, we might have noticed verses such as Genesis 3:19; Psalm 146:3, 4; Ecclesiastes 9:5; and 1 Thessalonians 4:13–17 that talk about death and the resurrection of the saints after Jesus returns. However, we did not realize that the church we attended, since childhood, not only perpetuated ignorance of the Bible in its members, but encouraged us to perform unbiblical rituals as a part of their central doctrine.

As a result, we anxiously awaited the arrival of a man who was supposedly endowed with heavenly powers. These powers came not from a connection with Christ, through faith, but because this peculiar character was in touch with deceased human beings that he claimed were saints.

I am thankful for Acts 17:30, which states, "Therefore having overlooked the times of ignorance, God is now declaring to men that all people everywhere should repent."

This was one of the times when my family and I were clearly ignorant of all the warnings against consulting with the dead (see Lev. 20:27; Deut. 18:11, 12; 1 Sam. 28:7; 1 Chron. 10:13; Isa. 8:19). With my lack of knowledge, I easily agreed with my mom.

> We frequently asked dead saints to intercede on our behalf in church, so it opened us up to being deceived in this way.

The healing man was blind, so my father left early that Sunday morning to bring him to our home. When Father finally arrived, he led a gray-haired, distinguished looking man into Mom's room. All the children were ordered to leave, but I pleaded to stay. My father gave me no argument.

My mom, of course, wanted a full explanation of what exactly he did. The man pulled out a simple, familiar prayer book and what looked like an ordinary key. He explained that he would place the key in the center of the open book and ask questions to discover the person responsible for my mother's illness. If the answer to the question was "yes," the key would turn in one direction. If the answer was "no," the key would turn in the opposite direction.

"But who do you talk with?" Mom asked, pointedly.

"Saint Anthony," the man replied.

After a prayer of invocation, the man proceeded to ask about my mom's past, including questions about her friends and enemies. Eventually, it came to light that one of my father's sisters was my mom's worst enemy. She was not only capable of harming her but also her entire family. When the key was asked if this woman was responsible for Mom's condition, it turned in the "yes" direction.

I was amazed. If I had not been in the room and watched it, I would have never believed it happened.

Aided by his strange device, the old man narrated Aunt Jezebel's malevolence toward our family. He explained that it started years ago, when she maliciously tried to rob my father of his land. After years of contention, the matter was taken to court and ruled in my father's favor. Outraged by the outcome, his sister sought revenge. She even admitted that she was responsible for my father's car accident.

The night before the accident, my mother had received a vision warning us of the dreadful incident. After relaying the matter to Father, she suggested that he not drive. Unfortunately, Father refused to heed the warning, and proceeded with his driving lesson. Mom remained at home deep in prayer. Although God allowed the accident to occur, He spared the lives of my father and brother. After a long recovery from a badly smashed leg, Father was almost as good as new.

According to the healing man, Aunt Jezebel's mischievous intent intensified when her plan was defeated once more. She summoned an evil spirit into my mom's life to torture her to death.

"Now," said the old man, "we can command this spirit out of you, but there is something you must know. In order to rid you of the spirit, I must return it to the responsible person."

"Oh, no," Mom interrupted adamantly. "That would be an act of revenge. What else can we do?"

"Well," answered the healing man, "We can command him out of you and give him no direction. That means he would be free to roam wherever he chooses. Chances are, however, he will return to you, or he may enter in any other member of your family."

After a long enough pause to ponder the two options, Mom spoke decisively. "I have no other choice but to send the spirit adrift and continue trusting in God's power to protect us."

Bitter moments of struggling and gasping for breath followed, while the healing man prayed for deliverance in the name of Saint Anthony. Finally, he announced that my mom was free. He explained that her struggle for breath was the result of the spirit making his exit through her nostrils.

I was comforted that my mom had been delivered from her affliction, but the morning's events left me perplexed. Mom slowly began regaining her strength and life returned to normal.

I returned to pursing my dreams. After all the interruptions, I resolved to concentrate all my efforts in pursuit of my goal. However, my thoughts kept replaying what I had witnessed. I reflected on the healing man and his little book constantly, whether alone or in a crowd. Sometimes, I had to abruptly close my eyes and pray to blot the scene from my memory. Still, the tormenting thoughts prevailed.

My nights grew restless, and I longed for the rescue of sleep. Then one night, the healing man appeared in my room. I had not been asleep, so it was not a dream. Neither was it visual hallucination; it seemed real to me. Although his face was not visible, I recognized the white shirt and black trousers he had worn during his visit. He held the little book in his left hand, but in the other hand was a whipping cord. As he lashed out at me with the cord, I did not experience the familiar sting; instead each lash was gradually choking me. It was a never-ending agony that left me gasping for breath. I repeatedly tried to scream for help only to discover I was speechless. I tried to get out of bed to go to my parents' bedroom or anywhere that could allow me to flee my unwelcome guest, but I was powerless to move.

After much anguish, I felt as if I were at the point of death. Then, the strange visitor disappeared in a flash. Frantically, I dashed for my parents' room and sprawled on the bed.

"Who is this?" Mom asked.

"That man," my trembling voice uttered in a whisper. "He tried beating me to death just when I was about to fall asleep."

I still wonder if Mom shared my thoughts that night: *Was I to be the next victim of that tormenting spirit? Was it a mistake for Mom to decline the chance of returning that evil spirit to its owner?*

After praying with me, Mom fastened a cross to my bosom to provide assurance of God's protection.

Ironically, the presence of the cross prevailed that night. After sobbing briefly, I peacefully fell asleep. However, my cross emblem was not always effective. That strange and dreadful visit by the healing man continued to return many other nights. I looked at the cross as my faithful companion, and sleeping with it often seemed to keep away my unwanted guest. After several nights without a visit, though, I took it for granted that his visits were permanently subsided, and I deliberately parted with the cross to prove my freedom.

I slumbered peacefully for several nights without the emblem, but then unexpectedly, the healing man made his appearance again and left me grasping for the cross. In addition, the cross was never a guarantee that the strange man would stay away. Many times, even the power of the cross was ineffective. After that first night, I did not want to share my experiences with my mom because I did not want her to feel guilty about it. I also did not want to encounter the healing man in person again. I feared that if I told my parents, they would call him to my rescue. I also hid the nighttime visits from my friends. I did not want any of them to think I was strange.

Although my biblical education had been poor to this point, I was always mindful that God was more powerful than any forces of evil. On this basis, it was convenient to trust in prayer. Still, beyond providing basic comfort, my prayers went unanswered until years later when I converted to the Seventh-day Adventist faith. This new life of faith and the prayerful intervention of Pastor Keith Dennis and Pastor Donte Tobias were finally effective in eliminating the healing man's intrusion in my life.

Chapter 9

My Angel Daughter

My eldest sister, Martha, who lived in Canada had suggested the name, Wanda Lisa, for my baby girl. From birth, my daughter resembled an angel. Some said she looked like me, others said she looked like her father, who finally made his way to my bedside in the hours following Wanda Lisa's birth. He was nine months and almost one day late, and he looked very perplexed during the visit. Beyond that, I was too preoccupied with my little one to notice what he said or did.

Despite her beautiful, angelic appearance, she looked so helplessly dependent on me and desperately in need of love and care. For a moment, I recalled and regretted my dismay over my unwanted and challenging pregnancy, but the joy I received from loving this child trivialized my troubles. I suddenly had nothing but her happiness in mind. For the second time, I was focusing on another person's needs instead of my own.

The doctors shared concerns they had about the soft spot on Lisa's skull. I was attentive to the medical advice. I was determined to comply with every instruction for my Wanda Lisa. In their guidelines, they did not inform me that her condition was fatal. No one prepared me for the worst.

As a result, the weeks and months following our discharge were punctuated with overwhelming discomforts and concerns. Wanda Lisa's head appeared to be growing much faster than the rest of her body and face, and the small, soft area in her skull became larger instead of smaller. She would sleep for hours and cry constantly in discomfort. We visited the doctor frequently, but that only added to my mental anguish. Despite my pleading, no medicine or interventions could be utilized for her cranial problem. The doctors refused to give me an explanation for the abnormality. In fact, the only thing I learned at each visit was the new size of her head, which was measured faithfully, and how to position it to lessen her physical discomfort.

The old adage, "A drowning man will clutch at a straw," describes my behavior at this point. I did not realize how public my plight had become until an older member of my church informed me that a woman named Mrs. Oliver* had offered to assist with Lisa's problem. I was not acquainted with Mrs. Oliver or the herbal therapy I was told she provided, but my desperation for a cure prompted an urgent

---

*   Name has been changed

response. I did not take the time to inquire about the woman or to even think about the ramifications of such a procedure. I am sure that discussing this matter with my seniors could have saved me not only time and money, but most importantly, unnecessary pain and suffering for Lisa. Determined to work against all odds to save my daughter's life, which I had become convinced was in grave danger, I only learned basic information from my friend about the therapist. She lived with her children and grandchildren a very long distance past our parish church, approximately sixteen miles from my home. Sixteen miles with St. Lucia's poor transportation and rugged, pothole strewn, public roads was a long distance. I could ride the bus for a short distance past the Parish church but then I would need to walk the remaining distance.

I still commuted to my full time job Monday through Saturday. I was grateful for my younger sister, who cared for Lisa during my absence. The end of every workday left me very exhausted but always eager to relieve my sister and devote my time to Lisa. Into my overworked schedule, I hurried to add in a visit with Mrs. Oliver. Without access to a telephone, I sent word by my friend.

The next Sunday, I boarded the wooden bus en route to the Parish church. Unlike the other passengers, my focus was not on church. I descended from the bus and headed up the winding, uphill path. After a few stops at some of the poorly kept cottages along the way, I finally reached my destination.

> # Again, I wanted to be in control of my daughter's fate. I wanted to save her.

Mrs. Oliver's place was no different from the other cottages. The children looked under nourished and had very large, distended stomachs underneath their tattered clothing. For an instant, I questioned the nature of my visit and the very thought of Lisa's exposure to such an environment, but the doctors had given me no other choice. My state of desperation left me vulnerable for exploitation.

Mrs. Oliver sold me on the idea of daily therapy, instead of weekend applications, to ensure its efficacy. In a matter of minutes, I agreed to place Lisa in Mrs. Oliver's care temporarily or until Lisa was cured.

"You are too young to be doing all this by yourself," observed Mrs. Oliver, sympathetic to the plight of a young mother. "I'll do my best for you."

The price for her generosity was $15 per week in addition to a supply of food and hygienic items, which I would bring on my weekend visits.

The first weekend I came to visit, I noticed Lisa's hygiene had been neglected. It was apparent that my innocence and vulnerability were being exploited. Hygiene and food supplies that would have lasted two weeks at home were completely depleted. I realized I needed to bring enough supplies to care for the other children as well. If I did not, my daughter's basic needs would be neglected. Still, I considered the end result of my daughter's health worth the sacrifice. So, instead of weekly visits, I committed to one to two visits during weekdays to make sure Lisa was receiving the best possible care. Thank goodness that Lisa's father was now in her life and helping with financial support.

My family did not approve of my decision, but I did not listen. I wanted to do all that I could for Lisa and the doctors offered me no more options. I would not just sit and watch her fade away. Again, I wanted to be in control of my daughter's fate. I wanted to save her.

My love for Lisa had no boundaries. In addition to the physical exertion to get there, my frequent visits were financially and emotionally exhausting. And on top of my busy schedule, my unwanted nighttime visitor continued to plague me. This combination created a constant state of tiredness.

I spent every dollar obtained from Lisa's father, and I depleted my own savings to zero. Thanks to my gracious sister, who allowed me to share her belongings and graced me with a few dollars between my paydays, I survived.

Had Lisa lived, she would be forty years old today. I do not regret my efforts to save her life. What I do regret is the fact that she died with unnecessary sores on her skull possibly from poor hygiene or strong herbal treatments. I also regret that she died away from those who loved and cared for her. When I realized my effort was hopeless and started considering my family's advice to bring Lisa home, the news reached me about her death. Stricken with grief and unable to face this reality, I considered Mrs. Oliver's offer to take responsibility for Lisa's burial. Many years later, I discovered Lisa's medical problem was hydrocephalus.

Although my memories of this difficult experience are still very emotional and overwhelming, it is not all negative. It still motivates my hope for the second coming. Although the most important incentive for heaven is my hope to see Jesus in person, the second most important desire is to reunite with my Wanda Lisa.

It is wonderful to think that my Lisa will be healthy, pure, and nothing less than an angel. In addition, my willingness to sacrifice my all in exchange for Lisa's life helped me understand, if not fully, how God's love for the human race was instrumental in the death of his Son. As children destined to die, God's love found a way to rescue us from eternal death.

"For God so loved the world, that He gave His only begotten Son, that whoever believes in Him shall not perish, but have eternal life" (John 3:16). This is one of the most quoted, but least understood verses in the Bible. We have a hard time comprehending the sacrifice of a child and the depth of love associated with it. Because of my experience with Wanda Lisa and the inspiration of the Holy Spirit, I have a clearer appreciation of this Scripture.

Chapter 10

Closed Doors are God's Opportunities

The effects of my wicked, destructive tumor caused such deformity to my face that, amidst all the painful circumstance in my life, I felt it was necessary to immediately implement Phase III.

Taking into consideration the hardships I encountered on the way to achieving my goal, I was reminded of my method to determine God's will for my life. When I viewed my efforts up to this point in light of the system I had created, the repeated struggles and disappointments within the past three years revealed God's disfavor with my plan.

Disturbed and disappointed, I again resorted to prayer. While asking God to show me His direction, I made sure to remind him that the matter was grave, and that He had promised to take care of me. I asked Him if relief from this marked plague was one of my greatest needs. My earnest question went unanswered.

I sank to a state of regret and helplessness, but as I passed the prime minister's office one gloomy day, I sought him out once again to speed any answer God might plan to give me. I reminded the prime minister of my long cherished dream and my dedicated efforts to accomplish that dream. I informed him that all my hard work had brought me to the point of disappointment and despair. Once again, my story brought about a compassionate response in him. He commended me for my persistence and fortitude, and then he promised to assist me. My heart filled with renewed hope, and I agreed to an appointment with him in one week.

To me this was a sure sign that God, in His goodness, had not entirely deserted me. It gave me a light at the end of the tunnel and hope for better days. At this point, not only was my faith renewed and my remorse replaced with gratitude, but I was convinced that Mr. Livingston had been divinely appointed to assist me with Phase III of my goal—entry to the United States of America.

A week later, I anxiously waited in the prime minister's office for the meeting that, in my imagination, would determine my destiny. As I waited, I began to ponder all the unnecessary toil and time I wasted with my own efforts to accomplish this goal. As I sat there in my enthusiasm, I came to the conclusion that Providence had predetermined this almost effortless achievement.

I was so lost in thoughts of my triumph that I jumped to my feet when the secretary called my name.

I entered Mr. Livingston's office apprehensively, but his warm, welcoming smile reminded me that not only was he in authority, but he had been divinely appointed to fulfill this mission. He had to hold the answer for which I had so long waited.

Mr. Livingston proceeded to tell me that the government would assist me financially with my flight and medical expenses, but I would need to have the surgery performed at the University of Medicine in Jamaica, which he described as equivalent to a United States hospital. He concluded that there was only one minor delay. Mr. Livingston was awaiting my doctors' response regarding the transfer of my case to Jamaica.

His favorable response was gratifying. I was speechless about the opportunity to fulfill my dreams, and felt overwhelmed with joy. This seemingly simple resolution had to be the answer to all my prayers.

Meanwhile, difficulty at my workplace was escalating. Not only was I not granted the increase in pay that was agreed upon hiring me for this new job, I was also humiliated by the unethical behavior of my boss. Upon hiring me, she promised to pay me more than others on my level, if I informed her of instances where staff were embezzling and shoplifting. I accepted the position, but I was not a private investigator. Nor was I raised to seek out coworkers and attempt to catch them doing wrong.

Despite knowing that I could not meet her demands for obtaining top pay, I expected her to at least pay me my worth. I was wrong. My failure to satisfy the constant inquiries she made forfeited any raises that I earned through hard work. By the end of my first year, I was still earning my initial pay without any promise of a better situation.

In anticipation of a new beginning, I decided to continue there until the time of my surgery, even though I felt uncomfortable. In fact, I already envisioned a successful surgery and speedy recovery. Now that I had all but achieved Phase III in my mind, I was looking forward to a new set of goals that were perhaps similar stepping stones for achievement – resume my education, become a qualified secretary, and become a civil worker. Once again, I could clearly see my future just as I had planned.

The very thought of handing my resignation to my present boss helped me tolerate my situation. With my surgery so near, I would no longer be the victim of ill will, unfair treatment, or an oblique future. I would not need to make the best of hardships anymore. My past and present turmoil became insignificant on the beautiful canvas I painted for my future.

With my dream dependent on word from the prime minister's office, I counted the days, watched my calendar, and too frequently checked with Mr. Livingston's secretary regarding any word from my doctor. Each time, I heard the disappointing, "Nothing yet."

At first, I reminded myself that it was just a matter of time and refused to be alarmed. When days of waiting turned to weeks, and weeks to months, it became difficult to remain optimistic. I was uncertain whether the doctor or the prime minister was at fault for the delay. I also began to suspect someone was misleading me.

"Dear Lord," I begged. "please don't let this happen. I can't take another closed door that appeared to be wide open."

I was finally summoned to the prime minister's office by a phone call from his secretary. I wasted no time responding to the request, and although the thought of a possible disappointment came to my mind, I refused to entertain it. Instead, all doubts were brushed aside with the thought that, after all, the God, who has brought me this far is very well able to see me through.

The prime minister called me in and read the letter from my doctor, who felt that the investment of time and money that would be required for the government's pursuit of my foreign medical procedures would end up a total waste. I half-listened to the letter, unwilling to face the dreadful conclusion. The prime minister read the last words penned by my doctor, which concluded succinctly that my sickness was untreatable.

When he finished, I sat motionless and speechless as my last ray of hope turned to despair. A dreadful fear enveloped my innermost being. I knew at that point that it was all over: the dream, the hope, and the bright, opportune future.

I sobbed there for a long time. Money, job, yesterday, today, tomorrow—I counted all of it lost. I had no desire to remain in the city any longer. My mind turned toward home in the country, where I belonged. It was then my resolve hardened to medical practitioners.

My thoughts ran wild. *I knew I should have never let those doctors near me. They've been liars all along. I will never set foot in that hospital again. If I must die, I'll die without giving them the satisfaction of experimenting with my face…*

In this frame of mind, I exited the dense and artificial air of Mr. Livingston's office, gasping for breath. The air outside did not seem to make a big difference. I felt like an intruder. I felt like I was standing on the outside of the world and looking in. As my thoughts continued to race, I concluded that I had no business there. Life was for people with hopes and dreams, not for me.

Because of my shallow faith, the circumstances of that day pulled a dark curtain over my mind. I could no longer see the working of Providence. I did not have hope or trust that God would prevail against all odds to fulfill the very thing I had always desired most. Although I had experienced small measures of faith throughout my life, I still did not understand that God's ways are not my ways, and His thoughts are not my thoughts.

The next day I quit my miserable job without explanation and prepared for departure to a new life of emptiness. I had no goals and no vision; I considered myself an occupant of space and nothing more. I did not want anyone to feel sorry for me, and hated to impose on others' happiness, even that of my own family. To prevent this, I braced myself to walk the last miles of life alone.

However, in the midst of all this darkness, I never felt totally alienated from God. It was obvious to me, though, that He was not the God I understood him to be. I even thought that perhaps for some reason, He did not want me to live.

I arrived at home in the country and no questions were asked. Living a double life with my family was never difficult. On the outside, I appeared to be basking in an atmosphere of peace and contentment, but I was miserable inside. They always perceived me as courageous and uncomplaining, so I superficially played up to their expectations and no one questioned me.

Living a life of deliberate, shallow faith made me very uncomfortable. I willed myself to be content with living in failure. I wanted to quit fighting, but something within me forbade my surrender. I longed to silence that inner force, but found it extremely difficult. It constantly reminded me that I was not a quitter and reproached me for self-inflicted severance from God. It nagged me because of my inability to trust Him. The utter feeling of helplessness was painful, but the absence of the peace that comes from taking God at His word and trusting Him to do what is best remained a constant torture.

One day, just to relieve my sense of guilt for doing nothing to help my family, or myself, I applied for a secretarial position with the largest Discount store in Castries. The pay for this position was modest, but if by chance I were hired, I could see the possibility of saving enough funds, within a year, to make a trip to the United States. Since I felt I had nothing to lose, I proceeded and was again affronted with the futility of my position. The interviewer told me without so much as a thought to my feelings that in spite of my qualification for the job, I could not be considered because of my facial deformity.

These were the coldest words ever spoken to me. I do not know how I was able to constrain my initial reaction. Thanking him for his candidness and his time, I excused myself. In that moment, something remarkable happened. Instead of feeling dejected or discouraged, a flame ignited inside me. I was motivated to fight, to live, and to hold the position of secretary, one day, if for no other reason than to prove this harsh interviewer wrong. I had no idea what caused my changed attitude; I just knew that I had to do it for my own satisfaction.

Perhaps it was this motivation to succeed that helped me decide to change my current situation without giving any thought to financial limitations or any other barriers. At this point I did not see myself being able to travel to the United States. With Martha's advice and her financial assistance, I decided to go to the neighboring island of Barbados instead. I thought perhaps some doctor there would give a more positive second opinion that could help me get back on track and achieve my goals. I did not really believe anything good would come from this. However, it was better than remaining home in the harmful stasis in which I was cocooned.

It was rather easy to make this decision. My savings of $325 was more than enough to cover the $80 airfare, and my cousin who resided in Barbados graciously welcomed me into her home for the duration of my stay. Immediately following my arrival, she secured a visit for me with the island's most renowned surgeon. In spite of her confidence in his ability, I did not share her optimism. My hopes had already been raised one too many times.

Since I had little enthusiasm about my visit, the doctor's shrewdness did not impress me. Also, his suggested treatment, which included slicing off portions of my buttock, sounded ridiculously inhuman. I had been down this road before, and it sounded like another experiment in which I would be the sacrificial guinea pig. Without allowing for me to comment, the doctor continued. His arrogance assumed my willingness.

"How soon can you be admitted?" the doctor asked. I was tempted to ignore him and see myself out the door, but for my cousin's sake, I felt obligated to respond politely.

"Well," I replied, "this involves a lot more work than I anticipated. I think it would be best if I talked it over with someone objectively before making a final decision. Let me discuss it with my cousin, and I will get back to you with my decision."

Beneath the surface, I did not think there was anything that would motivate me to give consent for such a torturous procedure.

"Call me when you're ready," the doctor yelled, as if he thought his crass behavior would bring me back. I turned and glared at him, hoping he could read my expression. I would never come back.

When my cousin inquired about the doctor's diagnosis, recommendations, and prognosis, I kept my response simple.

"The doctor is confident that he can do it," I said, "but I need some time to ponder his recommendations."

Without giving her time to inquire further, I quickly added, "I would rather not talk about it now. Do you mind?"

She must have sensed that I had been dissatisfied because she quickly reminded me of her fiancé's upcoming arrival from New York City. Her third application to the United States' Embassy had finally earned her a visa. She had been excitedly awaiting him, and anticipated that I, too, could come with them. While sharing her joy, I refused to share her optimism about the possibility of my acquiring a United States' visa. Even with assistance from her fiancé, I did not believe I would be able to travel with them to New York City in search of medical help.

If I had a stronger faith in the workings of Providence at the time, perhaps I might have seen her optimism as the opportunity to achieve my once cherished dream. However, for most of my life, I believed that God needed my assistance in order to grant my wishes. That was a terrible misconception. In His goodness, God showed me that worthy accomplishments are not the results of God, the Creator, depending upon humanity's actions. Our greatest accomplishments are the direct result of total dependence on Him.

> In His goodness, God showed me that worthy accomplishments are not the results of God, the Creator, depending upon humanity's actions.

Prior to the time when my dreams were crushed in Mr. Livingston's office, I pursued my goals relentlessly with painstaking efforts, unaware that I was trying to work through God instead of allowing God to work through me. It was not that God was shutting doors on my opportunities; instead, God was opening doors on His opportunities.

Looking back, I am amazed that a just and righteous God had so much love and mercy that He looked beyond my faults and my ignorance. He could have left me in my state of anguish and deprivation, but instead, with no conscious effort on my part, God worked through my cousin's fiancé and ushered me into the United States' Embassy. With less than $200 in my possession, I was able to secure a six-month visa upon my very first application, something unheard of in 1973.

Chapter 11

Between a Rock and a Hard Place

Although still enthralled by the circumstances initiating this accomplishment, I managed to entertain some thoughts about my United States adventure. I thought I was ready for it, but I was not. I had yet to learn an important lesson to prepare for the reformed life I was about to adapt after my emigration to the United States.

It was a beautiful day, and everything was going smoothly for me. My cousin and I spent the early morning hours strolling the warm sunny beach, stopping occasionally to welcome the gentle waves against our feet. Upon returning home, we engaged in a lavish brunch. Cousin Sue was famous for her stuffed flying fish and set a table fit for royalty. Following this luscious meal, we proceeded with packing my cousin's belongings. To explain the magnitude of this project, it is important to know that the packing began months before my arrival. Now, in spite of our combined, dedicated effort for the past three consecutive days, we were still far from completing the task.

Our departure to the United States was three weeks away, but we intended to spend two weeks of that time with our families in St. Lucia, so it was necessary to expedite this project. We also needed to prepare certain items for immediate shipment since Sue decided to ship them to St. Lucia and then be there personally to receive them in order to assure their safe delivery. To do this meant these assets needed to be shipped three days ahead of our flight from Barbados to St. Lucia. The only way to meet this goal was to continuously labor for it.

By the time Stan, my cousin's fiancé, entered the door and asked us out to dinner, we were extremely hungry and welcomed the invitation.

"Now, go and clean up," he commanded in his Barbadian accent. "I refuse to take out dirty women."

"Do you want to shower first?" Sue asked. "That will give me time to straighten up."

"Okay," I agreed, and proceeded to the bathroom.

My cousin's bathroom was designed with a wall separating the shower and commode from the powder room. That made it possible for me to take a shower and then use the powder area to get ready while Sue took a shower in complete privacy.

When I was finally able to take my place in the powder room while my cousin was in the shower I had nothing left to do but my hair. As I worked away, it seemed odd that Stan entered the room without knocking on the unlocked door. I scolded myself silently for being startled and stepped aside as he advanced toward the sink, thinking he must need to wash his hands. Then, without warning, he grabbed my arm, drew me to him, and kissed me on the lips.

I was too stunned to think of a clear response and watched in the mirror as he tossed a sly look my way before exiting. I was dumbfounded. *What have I done this time to deserve this?* I wondered, first examining my own behavior and then his. *What grave impudence that he should have the audacity to think that I am capable of deceiving my cousin who has been so dear to me?* Sue stepped out of the shower then, and I had to leave the room immediately lest she noticed my flushed face or shaking hands.

"I'll wait outside for you," I said over my shoulder.

There is nothing more distasteful than having a happy experience abruptly interrupted by something humiliating. I did not understand how this man who had so kindly assisted me in getting my visa to the United States suddenly felt he could pursue me like this.

Like a school of frightened fish, thoughts of Stan's intrusion pervaded my mind. I could not help but feel uncomfortable in his presence. It was only at the end

> Her last statement fell on my heart like a death-blow.

of the evening, when we got up to leave, that I was able to finally gain some relief. I needed peace and quiet to think about everything that occurred and therefore I carried my thoughts with me to bed. After tossing and turning for most of the night, I resolved to tell my cousin about the incident until I considered the hurt she would suffer from it. In the end, I decided it would be a battle I would fight on my own.

Unfortunately, I was no longer innocent to the ways of men. I knew exactly what Stan's motive was when he kissed me. This time, I would take action to prevent it from going any further. There would be no more treats or jokes, and I certainly would never allow myself to be alone with him, no matter what the circumstances. I could do this. We only had three days left until we would be heading home to St. Lucia. Once there, I knew we would go our separate ways until we went to the United States. Once in America, I would join my dear, sweet sister Martha and never have to spend time worrying about Stan again. Because the thought of seeing Martha after six long years revived my spirit, I steeled myself to survive this final ordeal.

The next day, my cousin informed me that she would be leaving me in the early afternoon. At the last minute, she decided to travel with her belongings to St. Lucia. I did not even attempt to hide my surprise and disappointment.

"I was lucky to obtain a seat," she added, trying to reassure me. "The boat was already overcrowded. Don't worry. Stan will stay here with you for the next two days, and he'll take you to the airport for your flight on Thursday."

Her last statement fell on my heart like a death-blow.

"But Sue," I responded, realizing she couldn't be spared the knowledge of her fiancé's deceitfulness and malevolence any longer. However, when I tried to explain what happened, she would not listen.

"Don't worry," she interrupted with utmost confidence. "Stan would never try seducing any relative of mine."

Oh, dear God! What have I done to deserve this? I wondered in despair.

The following two days were some of the longest and most laborious in my life. Keeping out of Stan's reach required my constant anticipation. I was continually in tune to his every move. For instance, I knew he usually left the house after breakfast at about 10:00 a.m. He didn't return until late afternoon. As soon as I saw his car approaching the driveway, I would rush back to my room.

Thankfully, the lock on my room could only be unlocked from the inside. Once behind those walls, I refused to exit until I had heard him go out the door the following day and watched his car disappear down the driveway. During the short hours of his absence, I ate sparingly, bathed, and attended to all my other essentials as quickly as I could, always listening for the car and keeping watch on the driveway.

The first night of my plan worked out better than I expected. Stan invited me to go out driving, but I was able to beg off through the door by explaining how tired I was.

The following morning he again knocked on my door and said, "Time for breakfast."

"I'm not hungry," I replied. "You go ahead."

I thought this day would work out as it had the day before, but Stan surprised me by coming home in the middle of the afternoon and insisting that I accompany him to dinner.

"Thanks, but I don't feel very well right now," I replied, safely behind the locked door of my room.

"All right," he responded. "I'll come back a little later, and then we'll go out to supper."

"Okay," I said, hoping to have another excuse by the time he returned, or better yet, I hoped he would forget his promise while roaming the streets.

Shortly after taking my seat next to the window in the late afternoon, the little red car came speeding up the driveway. Without a moment's delay, I rushed to my room and locked the door behind me. I held my breath as I heard Stan climbing up the stairway.

"Are you ready for supper?" he asked, knocking on the door.

"No!" I exclaimed. "I don't want to go anywhere with you."

I couldn't think of anything else to say to him.

"Why?" he asked. "I'm not going to eat you."

"I don't care," I replied. "Just leave me alone."

"Stay in there and starve then," he shouted as he stormed down the steps and slammed out the door. Peering from the bedroom window, I witnessed his car speeding down the driveway and onto the road. *Great,* I thought. *I just blew my cover.* Now that he knew I wasn't willing to cooperate my mind began to think about all the ways he could accomplish his intent by force. With nowhere to turn, I began to pray. I knew that the confrontation had just escalated to something beyond what I could handle on my own.

Once I finished, I realized that I needed to call for a taxi. I had to make arrangements to get to the airport the next day and break free of this house. Eager to escape my dilemma, I instructed the driver to report to my door at 6:00 a.m. It was four hours before my flight, but I was not about to miss my plane for any reason.

Once I had determined my plan, I began to prepare accordingly. First, I gathered all my belongings from the other parts of the house into my room while Stan was away. I quickly showered and then locked myself in my room and tried to sleep.

Too soon I heard Stan entering the house. Predictably, he did not leave me alone, but again came to my door. I tried to ignore the knocking, pretending I was asleep, but as it grew louder and fiercer, I began to fear he would break open the door. I lay trembling as if I were a little, frightened mouse before a hungry lion. I had nowhere to go and no one to turn toward. I knew I could pray, but I did not know what more I could say that had not already been said.

"Open up! Let me in!" Stan yelled. "I don't want to do anything to you. I know you're awake in there. Just think of all the trouble I went through to get your visa to the United States. Is this the gratitude I'm going to get from you? You'll have to find your own way to the airport if you don't open this door."

This monologue continued on for another twenty minutes before he let loose a string of obscene language followed by silence. Finally, he stomped down the stairs and again exited the house by slamming the door. I peeked out the window and watched as he left the yard.

"Lord, I hope he stays gone all night," I prayed.

My heart skipped a beat when there was a brisk knock on the door at 5:55 in the morning. A quick look out the window verified it was my taxi driver and not Stan. Grabbing my suitcase, I all but fled the house.

The pleasant taxi driver helped me into the car and carried on a friendly conversation with me all the way to the airport. As I stepped out of the cab at my destination, he commented, "I'm so glad you enjoyed your stay in Barbados. I hope you will come back soon."

I cringed inwardly, but politely said, "Thank you. I look forward to returning someday."

Hours later, as the aircraft soared into the lofty clouds, I was reminded of the obstacles I had encountered during my brief stay in Barbados. I noted God's intervention in my situation with Sue's fiancé. Not only was Stan forced out of the house, he didn't return.

Chapter 12

New York Struggles

On March 14, 1973, I finally entered the United States of America. This long-awaited opportunity was compounded with excitement and anticipation, but also apprehension. I worried about living in such a foreign environment, and I was sad to leave my family. With these mixed feelings, I entered New York City; it was both enchanting and overwhelming.

Growing up in St. Lucia, I heard many grand stories from others over the years about this famous city, though it is possible they had never even been there themselves. On the night of our arrival at Kennedy International Airport, it was all that I had dreamed. The enchantment of the city lights along with the lights of runway airport vehicles all amplified this deception.

Once we were on our way to Halsey Street in Brooklyn, the sites I saw no longer met my expectations. I blamed darkness for this until we stepped from the taxi outside Stan's apartment building. What I saw did not fit my mental image of the city.

"Let's call Martha!" Sue exclaimed after we entered Stan's apartment.

"Yes!" I responded enthusiastically.

I hoped my sister would come to my rescue that very night and put an end to my discomfort around Stan. Since there were two telephones, we were able to have a three-way conversation with my sister. We excitedly told Martha about the flight and our arrival. Sue spoke of how wonderful everything was, but I informed my sister that it had been a little disappointing. Sue was quick to inform me that once we saw the more beautiful areas, I would change my mind.

"Stan will take us sight seeing tomorrow," said Sue, "I can't wait."

"Are you coming tonight?" I asked Martha, ignoring Sue's remarks. I did not want to tell her that the reason I was unhappy with my surroundings was actually because of Stan.

"Tonight? No, not tonight," Martha replied. "But I can't wait to see you."

"I really want to see you, too."

"Actually, we're almost three hundred miles apart," Martha explained. "I have to take the bus or the train to get to you, and my work-schedule is not flexible. I'm not free until the weekend."

"Alright, I understand," I responded sullenly. "We'll see you on the weekend."

The following day, I awoke from a night of tossing and turning. Exhausted from the flight and the thought of spending four more days with Stan, I rushed to the window, eager for my first daylight view of New York City. What I saw in the morning light was shocking. I thought perhaps I was having a nightmare and had not woken up yet. There was garbage on the streets and children on their way to school wearing dirty jeans and tennis shoes. The sky was so gray that I wondered if it would storm. The people looked unsettled and moved throughout the streets quickly. This was not the magical city I had always imagined. Living my fantasy was gratifying, but confronting with the reality was very disappointing.

Inside the apartment, I knew I could not trust Stan, even with Sue present. However, on the first day, he did take us on a grand tour and taught us how to use all forms of public transportation. By the second day, we felt confident enough to go shopping without him. It was a thrill to shop in Manhattan and Delancy Street, and we joked cheerfully about not being able to find our way back home.

Elated by the day's activities, and grateful for our safe return, we were bursting with excitement as we tried on our ensembles and bragged about our adventure.

"You dummies!" Stan said laughingly. "You're not thinking. You bought all these winter clothes, and winter is almost over. You will need to store these for next winter and go back and shop for spring."

That might have been good advice, but my budget was tight and would not allow for purchasing any more clothing.

The following day, Sue wanted to look for work. Stan referred her to a number of agencies, and after several phone calls, they both left for interviews.

"Wish me luck," Sue said on her way out the door. "We need some more shopping money."

I wanted Sue to find a job quickly, but I dreaded that she would. If she went to work, it would mean I had to spend more time alone with Stan. I wanted her to wait until I left on the weekend, but I was silent. I gave her a hug and wished her well on her search.

In their absence, I tried writing to friends and relatives. Then I tried reading the paper, watching television, and eating, but I could not help being reminded of the possibility that Sue might go to work. If that happened, I would be left to face another Barbados experience in an apartment that had no locked room for safety. Distressed, I resorted to prayer.

"Please, Lord," I sobbed, "don't allow me to relive that. I'm so tired. I feel incapable of fighting physically or mentally. You must come to my rescue. Don't let Sue go to work before I can leave this place."

I must have sobbed myself to sleep because I was awakened by the sound of a key joggling in the keyhole. Before Sue could speak I knew what had happened.

"You got the job?" I forced myself to ask.

"Yes!" she exclaimed. "It's a living-in job, but I have to start from somewhere."

"When do you start?" I asked apprehensively.

"I go in on Sunday," Sue replied. "She wanted me to start immediately, but I managed to convince her to wait until then. I thought that would give us a little more time for sight-seeing before you leave for Hartford."

"Oh, you're so thoughtful!" I exclaimed. "It isn't any wonder that you're my favorite cousin."

Though I meant the compliment sincerely, I realized that Sue's actions were the direct result of God's intervention in answer to my prayer. I silently thanked Him for granting my request.

The following days were wonderful. We spent time visiting with old acquaintances we had not seen in years. Finally came the glad day of Martha's arrival. I wished I could hurry the hours and I found myself continuously checking the time every ten or fifteen minutes. At last there was a knock on the door and a familiar face through the keyhole.

A joyous reunion followed. We talked and laughed tirelessly. If Martha noticed the increasingly effects of my illness, she did not mention it. Instead she told me we would find the best doctor capable of providing the necessary treatment. Martha had always made it so easy for me to depend on her. However, her next statement crushed me.

"I'm sorry I can't take you back with me this weekend," she said. "I'll have to come back for you in two weeks."

"But why?" I asked, trying to conceal my disappointment.

"Well," she replied, "my living arrangements aren't adequate right now. In fact, my roommate is kind of grumpy, and I don't want her making things uncomfortable for you. I'm going to find us a little place of our own where we can really feel at home."

I wanted to beg her to take me with her, but instead I agreed. The conversation moved on to the experiences she had been through since her emigration and how things were at home. I could not help but tease her about the way she was dressed. She had always been modest, but now she wore a long skirt with no adornment.

I even laughed and joked claiming that she must have gotten her style from an old woman. We thought that we would celebrate by returning to the shopping district, but Martha refused to join us. I had hoped to introduce her to real style.

Later I discovered that our reunion had not been entirely happy on her part. She was very worried about me, both for my physical and spiritual wellbeing. While Sue and I shopped, she remained home to pray. Although I would not have been receptive to all her concerns at the time, I am thankful for her prayers, and for the way God worked wonders in my heart during the following weeks.

Our weekend was fun, but in my mind it was clouded by the coming separation. Sunday rolled around and both Martha and Sue were leaving me alone with Stan. This time, I did not pretend to be unaffected. In fact, fighting back the tears was impossible. Sue, undoubtedly, shared my discomfort about being left behind and promised to call me every night until her return.

"Stan is going to ride the train with me to work. You can come with us," she suggested. "You can get something to eat together on the way back."

"It has been an emotional day and I think I'm ready for an early night," I said. "Do you mind if I stay home?"

I hated to turn her down, but I needed some time alone to contemplate my defensive strategy against her fiancé. My bedroom was the couch in the living room. As I tried to think of a way out of my predicament, I fell asleep.

I awoke to the phone ringing. Martha called to reassure me that she would hurry in her task to bring me to her. When she hung up, Sue called to tell me goodnight. She was disappointed that Stan had not returned and I was alone, but secretly I was happy and prayed he would remain gone for the entire night. After the calls, I again fell asleep.

When I awoke once more, something about the dawning of the new day chasing away the fearsome night seemed magical. Amazed that my night had been so peaceful, I tiptoed past the half-opened door of the only bedroom and caught a glimpse of the vacant bed. Unwilling to accept that sole piece of evidence that my prayers had been answered, I knocked repeatedly before entering the bathroom to avoid unwelcome surprises. In the kitchen, everything was still placed in the order that I left it. I had spent the night alone.

Elated and encouraged by this direct evidence of providential care, I had no reason for further dismay. With a sense of freedom, I accomplished the few activities of my day, and soon ended up writing letters and staring out the window at cold Brooklyn streets. I knew this could never be my second home and longed to be with my sister.

Again I found myself idle, so I turned on the television and became involved in the soap opera, *Days of Our Lives.* However, as the story unfolded, revealing its array of fornication and adultery, an unusual feeling of discomfort disturbed my conscience. I tried to ignore it, but there was no silencing the small voice that spoke against what I saw.

As I gave way to the inner voice, I saw Stan's intent to seduce me replicated throughout the soap opera. I began to question how I could hate a situation in real life while being entertained by it on television. I wondered if watching these things could eventually make me numb to them in real life. My powerlessness against Stan compelled me to turn off the television. I reaffirmed my determination to never again be a victim of non-consensual sex.

With nothing else to do, I picked up my Bible. Reading God's Word prayerfully seemed like the ideal weapon for my anticipated battle with Stan. As usual, I turned to the comforting and familiar Psalm 23. I realized that the God whom the author trusted was the same God who cared and guided me throughout my life's journey. After reading this encouraging passage, I heard Stan's footsteps approaching the door.

"Where have you been?" I demanded. I was determined not to shrink in Stan's presence. After all, I had God on my side. "Sue called and was surprised to learn that you have not been home since she left."

"Never mind her!" he responded. "I'm here now. Did you miss me?"

"I'm sure you know the answer to that question," I replied.

Ignoring the implication of my statement, he advanced in my direction and invaded my personal space.

"If you don't stay away from me, I will be forced to call the police," I told him.

"You'd be wasting your time," Stan sneered. "This is New York City. They won't believe a word you say."

It was true that what I had seen of New York had given me the same impression, but I was not about to be manipulated into passivity. Stan began his advance again, but in that instant, the thoughts of my first sexual encounter flashed before my eyes. Anger burned inside me and aided me in the most gruesome physical fight of my life as I resisted Stan's advances. The struggle seemed as if it were a long nightmare, but eventually my opponent surrendered.

"Horse!" Stan spat as he stalked off to his room.

Ordinarily, such an accusation would have insulted me, but considering the situation, I was glad that he recognized my ability to fight and hoped he would not want to repeat it.

Sadly, I was again attacked later that day, but again I fought and triumphed. My sudden display of repulsion and physical strength was unlike me. It had always been my younger sister who was my bodyguard against any school bullies. I began to wonder if the real me was this strong, violent woman and feared it for a moment. Then I realized that if I gave Stan the slightest hint of weakness, it could result in my defeat, so I concealed my fears.

> ## His maneuvers are not always explicit, but the outcomes are always right.

The remaining hours of the evening were filled with fear and frustration. I was unable to sleep and spent the night praying that the Lord would get me out of there. I know it was one of the most sincere prayers I ever prayed.

When the phone rang, I leapt to my feet, hoping it was Martha.

"Pick up the phone, Rita," Stan said in a sweet voice, as if we were having a wonderful time together. My prayers again had been answered. Martha's voice came clearly through the phone.

"Did I wake you up, sugar?" she asked soothingly.

"I wasn't asleep," I replied.

"What were you doing?" she wondered.

"I was just lying on the couch thinking about everything," I responded.

"Would you be scared to take the bus by yourself to Hartford?"

"Scared!" I exclaimed, my heart beating rapidly in anticipation. She had no idea that I was more scared not to take a bus to Hartford. "You just tell me how, and I'll show you how scared I will be."

"Well, I know you're not scared," Martha said, "but I don't want you to get lost in that huge bus terminal. I asked Stan to put you on the bus for me. Once on board, don't get off until you get to Hartford's Greyhound Bus Terminal where I will be waiting for you."

I bit my lip so I would not ask her why she had involved Stan. Instead, I replied, "That's just wonderful! I can't wait!"

Everything was confirmed. My time of departure from the Greyhound Bus terminal in Brooklyn, my arrival time in Hartford, my pre-paid fare, and Stan's promise to get me to the Brooklyn terminal.

I wanted to sing praises for the perfection of God's strategies in leading me through this time. His maneuvers are not always explicit, but the outcomes are always right. Such a revelation of God's loving care relieved my aching heart.

I should have been able to sleep after the wonderful call that laid out my deliverance, but the thought of the raging wolf in the bedroom reminded me of the possible danger that still lurked. I tried to remain awake and alert. Despite such determination, nature proved a winner at some point, for my next moment of consciousness was the welcome light of a new day.

Now, that's another miracle, I thought, as I sprang to my feet, eager to pack, say good-bye to New York City, and close another chapter of my life struggles. As I went about my business, I kept Stan in my peripheral vision. He remained silent as he helped himself to breakfast. For once, he did not bother me. I began to wonder if he was angry enough that he would refuse to take me to the terminal. Of course, the bus was not scheduled to leave until early afternoon. So, I had plenty of time.

When Stan left that day without saying a word to me about where he was going or whether he would be back on time to see me to the bus terminal, I braced myself for the challenge of the day. Without any further delay, I began planning the journey. Although the train station was within walking distance, I considered taking a taxi since I was carrying two suitcases. Thankfully, Sir had given good instructions for navigating America when I was a child. "If your future places you in a foreign country and you are in need of directions, be sure to inquire of people in uniforms such as guards and police officers and never trust ordinary people."

With my bags packed and my plan made, I sat quietly waiting until it was time for my departure. Between my watch and the clock on the wall, I knew the correct time, but still I wondered what was wrong. Minutes appeared to last for hours, and hours seemed like days.

In the midst of this frustration, I heard familiar footsteps in the hallway. At the sound of the key in the keyhole, disappointment filled me. I had assumed that like the situation in Barbados, Stan would remain gone until after my departure, but there he was, looking rather pleasant and pretending to be innocent of his lewd conduct. I decided to give him the benefit of the doubt; perhaps he had experienced a change of heart. Then he stepped closer, grabbed me, and tried to kiss me. I managed to jerk away from him.

"What will it take for you to give up, Stan?"

He paid no mind to my question and darted toward me, capturing my hand. Then, he dragged me to his bedroom and threw me on the bed.

"Do you think I'm gonna go through all this trouble to get you up here just so you can get all fixed up and return home to your boyfriend?" he demanded.

Again, the physical struggle between us resumed and continued for what seemed to be a long time. When I felt as if I would never win against his strength and considered surrendering to the inevitable, scenes from my first rape flashed before me. I recalled how passively I responded to the matter because of my fear and pride. This thought kindled so much anger in me that I found myself not just fighting Stan, but also my first attacker.

At this point, Stan reached for his gun from underneath the pillow. Shoving it in my right ear, he insisted, "You either give it up, or you are dead."

"You might as well shoot," I responded, holding still lest the gun accidentally discharge. "But just be prepared to answer to my family."

For two minutes, we stared at each other in silence. For two minutes, the cold steel of the gun pressed itself into my ear. And for two minutes, I held as still as I could, barely allowing myself to breath. Then Stan stood and exited the room so suddenly that it made me flinch.

"Find your own way to the bus terminal!" he roared.

I laid on the bed, motionless, until I heard the door slam.

Relief flooded my body. Again, I knew I had been spared. I managed to pull myself to my feet. I was exhausted from the mental and physical exertion. I knelt to give thanks to God, but ended up just crying. I pictured my mother praying over me as she had done many times before, and the thought soothed my anguish. We may have been thousands of miles apart, but I felt I could rely on her prayers. Her last words to me before I left came to mind, "I will continue praying for you, so don't worry about anything."

I stood and looked at the clock, realizing I needed to hurry. When I arrived at the first train station, I was careful to write down every detail the man in uniform there gave me. Then I rehearsed the directions until they were in my memory so I would not seem uncertain of where I was and be an easy prey for malicious people.

Once in the bus terminal, I found another man in uniform to locate my Greyhound bus connection. I checked with the bus driver, who assured me he would inform me of my destination in Hartford, Connecticut. Taking my seat, I finally felt safe enough to relax. I closed my eyes and basked in the near fulfillment of my fondest dreams.

Chapter 13

New Horizons

Martha had informed Mrs. Stein, her employer, of her need to return to Canada in order to assist me with my medical needs. Not wanting to part with Martha's dedicated and devoted services as a babysitter and housekeeper, Mrs. Stein offered assistance.

"I am quite sure we can help your sister," she concluded.

When I arrived in Hartford that evening, Mrs. Stein approached Martha after speaking with her husband.

"Tomorrow I will call and make an appointment for your sister with Dr. Paul Rafetti," Mrs. Stein said. "He is a renowned plastic surgeon at Mount Sinai Hospital. He is a caring, reputable surgeon. Your sister will be in good hands."

"But how will we pay for it? We have no insurance," Martha reminded her.

"No problem," replied Mrs. Stein. "My father-in-law practically built Mount Sinai Hospital. You will see his name on almost every wall. Just tell them my husband will be responsible for everything, and let them know that they may forward any of the necessary documents to his office for his signature. He will sign and return them promptly."

The whole thing sounded too good to be true, but we later learned that the elder Mr. and Mrs. Stein were key builders of Mount Sinai Hospital and the younger Steins were among Hartford's most influential millionaires. They had earned the respect of the Mount Sinai Hospital staff through their generous financial support.

Mount Sinai was a wonderful hospital and Mrs. Stein was placing me in the hands of not only one of the most effective plastic surgeons but also caring nurses and other wonderful staff. I was even driven to my first medical appointment in the Stein's chauffeur driven Cadillac.

During my visit, it was time to answer what seemed to be a million questions about my case in order for Dr. Rafetti to make the assessment. I brought my sister, but unlike my former doctors, I liked Dr. Rafetti from the start and was comfortable with him.

At the end of the examination, he escorted me to the waiting room and returned to his office to consult with my sister. To this day, I am unsure if she told me everything he discussed with her in private. However, I know that any information she withheld was done with the best intentions. She did respond to the questions I had afterward by explaining that the doctor was concerned about the gravity of the tumor not because of its nature but because it had grown.

On the days that followed, I underwent painful tests in the radiology department. Dr. Mosquitz, chief of radiology, had advanced toward the car upon my arrival. He and his staff gave me such a warm welcome that I kept my fears silent as he gently informed me of the unavoidable pain and discomfort I would need to suffer for the procedures. The crew of male staff surrounded me, ready to apply pressure to any and all of my body parts that might jerk or move and interfere with the process. He told me that any movement on my part would not only interfere with the tedious procedure but might also cause them to have to repeat the procedure and could delay my treatment.

Through all this, I simply smiled and asked no questions about what might occur. He was slightly perplexed by my response, but soon developed the opinion that I was quite courageous. This was confirmed when I remained motionless through the painful procedures. Tears streamed down my face unrestrained, but I neither complained nor moved. Dr. Mosquitz and his team were a band of angels.

> She reminded me that my Father in heaven was rich, and as a child of God, I had access to all according to God's will.

They performed the painful procedures while continually regretting and apologizing for my discomfort. Their kindness increased my resolve to win the fight. After a number of tests and X-rays, I was finally left to ponder the results.

Outside of the hospital procedures, I struggled internally with my new lot in life. In a matter of days, I went from being a poor nobody to being someone who mattered. I felt undeserving and intimidated by all the wealth that surrounded me. When I discussed my discomfort later with Martha, she reminded me that my Father in heaven was rich, and as a child of God, I had access to all according to God's will.

"You can hold up you head and walk with your back straight," she told me.

It was after she said these words that I noticed Martha had a habit of walking with her head up high and her back straight.

When Dr. Rafetti's office called to confirm our appointment to hear the prognosis, Martha and I probably shared the same thoughts. Was the tumor benign or malignant? What new procedures would I need to endure? Without expressing any of these questions, we both agreed that we would think positively and anticipate a good report.

It was obvious when we entered the doctor's consultation room that Dr. Rafetti thought his report was excellent. He shared the good news that the tumor was benign; it had not penetrated my skull or entered my brain.

Because of this, surgical procedures and expected results were favorable. I would need to have at least three surgeries to remove all the affected tissue. I was not as optimistic as my doctor once everything was explained. My high hopes and expectations left no room for the unpredictable number of surgeries needed to correct the deformity, followed by several cosmetic surgeries. In addition to extensive skin grafting from other body parts, which would leave scars, the procedure on my face itself would leave an obvious and undesirable facial scar.

The procedure that Dr. Rafetti explained was similar to the one described by the surgeon in Barbados. I had refused that surgery in order to come to the United States, a land that offered a promised cure according to my dear principal those many years ago. Even in this land of promise it seemed I was being told the same thing: do not expect a miracle. In my mind, I thought I would be offered a cure that left no trace of disfigurement. It had become painfully obvious that I should be thankful to receive the cure alone regardless of any ill effects that might come with it.

With this knowledge, I consented to begin the medical procedures in one month. The time between was necessary so that the doctors here could receive my past medical records to help them better understand the early nature of my pervasive facial tumor.

The period of waiting and anticipating would be difficult, but it was supported by Martha's faith. Shortly after Martha's emigration to Canada, she wrote to tell us about her conversion to the Seventh-day Adventist faith. In fact, she had some interest in this faith since her early teens. Our whole family was very upset that Martha had turned her back on our Catholic faith, especially for a church that seemed so foreign.

On the first Saturday that she invited me to her church, I went simply because I did not want to disappoint my kind sister. Besides, I saw no harm involved in going to one service. It would be my first and last visit. I was willing to accept her right to believe whatever she wanted, but *I* was going to retain my own Catholic faith. Granted, I had some objections to certain practices and teachings of Catholicism, but I never felt pressured to follow them.

Having established in my mind that Martha's religion was inferior, I was ready to pick out any of their "erroneous" doctrines. One matter of contention was clearly the dress code. Not only were the women to dress modestly in skirts that went below the knee, but they were not allowed extensive makeup, jewelry, or body piercings.

Until then, I viewed all this as a joke. However, being the only person in the audience wearing a mini-dress, makeup, and jewelry, I felt the joke was on me. I was embarrassed, humiliated, and out of place. The people around me seemed to have realized that no matter what you do to your outside to dress it up it would not change what was on the inside. The difference between us was evident to everyone, and I felt strangely out of place.

No, I rationalized to myself, *I'm not strange. I only feel this way because I'm in the presence of some strange people.*

With this self-flattering thought, I hoped to ignore the apparent Godly influence of this environment. Still, I found it difficult to ignore the warmth, welcome, and kindness expressed toward me by both church members and the clergy. They conveyed a message of love that was very impressive.

Later, as I reflected on the service, I noticed that everything about the worship setting was soul searching and inspiring. Their praying was not repetitious. There were no recitations addressed to the Blessed Virgin Mary or any other saint. Prayers were directly offered to God the Father through the name of His Son, Jesus. They made me feel as if I were in the presence of the Lord.

The Bible was read in plain English and the passage was then discussed to help me understand and apply it to my life.

I did not miss the absence of the Latin language, nor did I miss the statues of the saints. In fact, the clarity of the service made statues unnecessary. Even a child would be able to learn from this. I was blessed. I shook the minister's hand on the way out, silently conceding that the service had been good, but reaffirming that I would not be giving up my Catholicism.

I was vaguely familiar with the Seventh-day Adventist religion prior to coming to the United States. However, my association with it had been minimal and had only served to create negative stereotypes in my mind. There had been one Adventist family in my neighborhood growing up. One daughter was a "Miss Perfect," very self-centered and egotistical, and refused to even greet us, much less talk with us. Her biological brother was not only promiscuous, but my dreadful rape, at age fourteen, was perpetrated by him.

It was probably because of this prejudice that I was determined to turn down Martha's second invitation to church. My sister was filled with kindness, thoughtfulness, and concern for me. She even presented me with a gift of a very flattering ensemble.

"Why did you do this?" I asked. "I don't want you spending all your money on me!"

I felt that her generosity obligated me to attend her strange church even if I would never become one of the dreadful people it contained.

"It's no trouble," she said. "I came across this little dress on sale. It looked so much like you, and then I managed to get the hat, shoes, and purse to match. I thought you would like it."

I could not object to such courtesy. When I tried the new outfit on, everything fitted perfectly. I could do nothing more than thank her for the gift and reiterate my concern for her overspending.

This deed of kindness motivated my visit to her church. As before, I vowed to stay aloof and told myself again that this would absolutely be my last visit. I had much better things to do with my time, so they better count it a privilege to have me.

As the worship service unfolded, I found myself inspired and involved. Again, I found myself responding positively and against my will to the service. I have since decided that in the same way the sick do not refuse medicine and the lonely child does not refuse love and affection, I sought the spiritual food the Seventh-day Adventist Church could provide.

My Savior, in His mercy, looked beyond my self-erected walls and loved me enough to draw me into His arms. He could have passed me by while I stood there, determined not to yield to the altar call. But as a loving and gentle shepherd, Jesus did not turn away. His soothing voice assured me that He who had accompanied me all through life's toil was calling me to experience the heights and depths of His love.

Even with this urgency inside me, I wanted to postpone my conviction. I turned to Martha with teary eyes and inquired, "Should I go to Him?"

"It's your decision," Martha replied.

At the pastor's softly spoken invitation, I could no longer resist. An awkward feeling came over me as I took my first step in the pastor's direction, but as I continued walking, I envisioned Jesus standing in the minister's place, and my fears and doubts were suddenly replaced by courage and hope. Relieved and elated, I stood there sobbing while the pastor prayed about my life. I was now committed to walking with Jesus all the way.

This was the first of two transcending experiences of my life. The gift of eternal life, eternity with Christ, and the family of God became my central focus as I stood pondering the love of God for me demonstrated in John 3:16.

"Lord," I responded to the call, "I believe what you are offering is much more than the best of this present life. Like you, I am willing to give my life as a sacrifice if it means that doing so will help somebody accept your gift of eternal life."

Although I later wondered why I made such a commitment when I was not equal to Christ's sacrifice, I feel that God answered my questions decades later.

Afterward, I was ready to embrace my sister's faith with open arms. Having discussed my wishes with Martha, I was informed that the next step would be baptism by immersion. Once completed, I would become an official member of the church.

"When will that be?" I inquired.

"Perhaps a couple months," she told me.

"Why such a long wait?" I asked.

"There is a baptism scheduled in two weeks," Martha explained, "but you probably will not be able to do that one simply because you won't be adequately educated by then. Bible study is a very important prerequisite for baptism."

Foremost in my mind was my upcoming surgery. I was very disappointed that I could not be baptized before my ordeal began.

A warm welcome was extended to me, as the man who was soon to be my favorite elder escorted me into the new believers' class. The absence of skepticism and disbelief made it easy for me to understand and accept the Bible truths presented. The Bible came to life as never before. Every word read affected my yearning heart like refreshing rain on parched, desert land. At the end of the session, Elder Earl told me how impressed he was with my comments.

"Do you come from an Adventist background?" he inquired.

"Unfortunately, not," I replied. "I'm new to all of this."

"It's hard to tell," he continued. "Your comments are well in line and very thought provoking."

I did not quite know what to think of his statement, but it impressed me to take advantage of the opportunity and express my concern to be a part of the upcoming baptism. I let him know that I felt the need to experience baptism before my first surgery. To my surprise, he did not object. In fact, he promised to take my request to the pastor and have an answer for me by the end of the worship service.

In spite of his positive response, I realized that my request was not normal protocol and could only be possible if God willed it. So, I prayed about it repeatedly.

"Lord," I prayed, "I feel that You've been with me all my life even when I didn't recognize You. Now that You have brought me this far, I ask You to allow my inclusion in this early baptism. If You will it, I will see it as a sign of Your approval and acceptance of my commitment to continue my walk with You by way of this faith.

At the end of the service, I was called to the pastor's study. There in the presence of the elders, he explained to me the prerequisites of baptism. Not failing to express his understanding of my request, he further explained that it would be to my advantage to take time and ponder my decision before engaging in baptism.

In my thoughts, Jesus has been walking with me all my life. I knew that He had led me to this place for the purpose of going all the way with Him. There was no reason on my end to wait, but I agreed to do just that.

The following day, I received a call from Elder Earl, who informed me that the pastoral staff had further discussed my request. They had agreed to grant me early baptism if I could correctly answer all the questions pertinent for a Seventh-day Adventist baptismal candidate. He reminded me that acknowledgement of these beliefs was an essential prerequisite for every candidate for baptism. After consenting to the test, it occurred to me that I did not have any idea as to what the questions were. I was trusting in the wisdom of an all-knowing God and that is what made me optimistic.

At the time, I only knew what I believed. Now that I have had years to explore my faith, I can provide solid scriptural responses for each of the areas where I was questioned.

- I believe in the Godhead, or Trinity, which consists of the Eternal Father, the Lord Jesus Christ, the Creator and redeemer of men, and the Holy Spirit (Matt. 28:19; 1 John 5:7).
- I believe that the Holy Scriptures of the Old and New Testaments were given by the inspiration of God and are the only unerring rule of faith and practice (2 Tim. 3:15, 17).
- I believe that every person must experience the new birth to experience salvation (John 3:17; Matt. 18:3; 2 Cor. 5:17).
- I believe in baptism by immersion that occurs after one has been taught the gospel, believes in Christ as Lord and Savior, repents of all sins, and makes their confession (Matt. 28:19; Mark 16:16; Acts 2:38; Rom. 10:10; Rom. 6:16; Col. 2:12).
- I believe that the Ten Commandments are God's moral law, binding for all men in all ages (Exod. 20:3–17; James 2:10, 12).
- I believe that the fourth commandment of the Decalogue requires the observance of the seventh-day Sabbath, which is a memorial of creation and a sign of sanctification (Gen. 2:2; Exod. 10:8–11; Ezek. 20:12; Luke 23:56).
- I believe that man by nature is mortal (Job 4:17) and God "only hath immortality" (1 Tim. 6:16).

- I believe that immortality and eternal life are the gift of God and are received only through Christ (Rom. 6:23; 2 Tim. 1:10).

- I believe that man's condition in death is that of unconsciousness. The dead, both good and evil, remain in the grave until their resurrection. None go to heaven or hell at death (Eccl. 9:5, 6, 10; John 5:28, 29; 1 Thess. 4:16, 17; 1 Cor. 15:51–53).

- I believe that hell will be a real lake of fire where all sinners will be burned up, utterly destroyed, and cease forever to exist (Rev. 20:13, 14; Psalm 37:20; 2 Thess. 1:9).

- I believe in supporting the gospel through tithes and offerings (Mal. 3:8–11; Matt. 23:23; 1 Cor. 9:9–14).

- I believe that the second coming of Christ is very near, and that it will be literal, personal, and visible to all (John 14:1–3; Acts 1:9–11; Matt. 24:30; Luke 21:27–31; Rev. 1:7).

- I believe in the ordinance of humility and the Lord's Supper (John 13:1–17; 1 Cor. 11:23–26).

- I believe that a follower of Christ should regard his body as the temple of the Holy Spirit and therefore abstain from all intoxicating beverages, tobacco, coffee, unclean meats and every soul defiling habit and practice (1 Cor. 3:16, 17; 9:25; 10:31; Prov. 23:29–32; Deut. 14:3–20; Isa. 66:15–17).

- I believe that the followers of Jesus should manifest true Christian modesty in dress and deportment, and should shun all questionable, worldly amusements such as the theater and dance (1 Tim. 2:9, 10; Matt. 24:37–44; James 1:27; 2 Tim. 3:4, 5).

- I believe in the gifts of the Spirit including the spirit of Prophecy (Eph. 4:8–11; Rev. 12:17; 19:10).

With each question I answered, Elder Earl's faced looked pleased. Then, there was a sudden hush. Amazed, I looked around me only to notice the shaking of heads.

Oh, Lord, I thought, *what have I done?*

It was then that Elder Earl came forward, took me into his arms, and told me I was a miracle.

"You've answered every question correctly," he said. "We have no reason to delay your baptism."

Convinced that this was another miracle on my behalf, I vowed to remain true to my commitment. On the following Saturday, I was privileged to experience the transforming power of grace and baptism by immersion. Contented and at peace, I entered the hospital on the following Monday, fearless but prayerful.

Chapter 14

Weathering the Storms

My medical procedures began in 1973, shortly before my twenty-first birthday. It was an inspiring time in my life, and I met some very special people. These friends strengthened my determination and will to live in ways that were very similar to those used by my schoolmaster during my adolescence. These messages of hope, courage, and well wishes were expressed through cards, gifts, prayers, visits, services, and in personal conversations. With providential intervention working through so many wonderful people, what could have been an anxious, bitter experience turned out to be forever gratifying.

The staff members of the Mount Sinai Hospital were a gift from God. I still have enjoyable flashbacks of the chief radiologist's daily visits and his cheerful demeanor. The nursing staff was no exception in this display of kindness. I do not recall ever even ringing my bell. Their constant attention to my needs and discomfort did not make it necessary. Because of excessive swelling of both eyelids, I had no vision for several days. This time of physical darkness was enlightened because I was touched and influenced by so many positive people including my new church family. I was told later that their prayers continually ascended to heaven. The Stein family, of course, left their imprint on my life by their kind deeds that opened the door to all these remarkable memories.

The day of my discharge was highlighted by Dr. Mosquitz's broad smile, well wishes, and comments about my bravery. He presented me with a little book titled *Jonathan Livingston Seagull* and an impressive clock radio. He explained that I still had far to go in life and that I should never give up on my dreams. He told me that the clock would help me to keep up with time so I could accomplish everything. His perception of me had a very positive influence on my life.

One of the most inspiring memories of this experience involved my sister Martha. She told me the phone rang several hours after my first scheduled surgery while she was, again, on her knees praying.

"Come, Martha," Mrs. Stein said, anxiously handing her the telephone. "It's Dr. Rafetti!"

"It's all out," the doctor informed her in his calm, assuring voice. "We took it all out with the first surgery, and it is not cancerous. Further surgery will only be cosmetic, but the tumor is all out."

When my sister heard this, she realized her prayers had been answered for more than she had asked. She wanted my safety through the procedure and those to come, and God in His infinite beneficence had provided not only that, but also assured that I would not need any more surgeries to remove the growth.

Isaiah 65:24 states, "It will also come to pass that before they call, I will answer; and while they are still speaking, I will hear." This verse was, and still remains, a stronghold for Martha and me during the difficult, stormy times of life.

Doctor Rafetti, meanwhile, had become attached to me as a surrogate father figure. When he discovered that I did not have occupation, he offered me a live-in babysitting job only a few months after my first surgery. I gladly accepted his offer.

"Good!" he exclaimed. "With the new baby and our two- and three-year olds, my wife could use some extra hands. You can earn some money instead of staying home alone and getting bored."

Although he did not mention it at the time, his offer also included two other generous, significant benefits: he provided me with medical insurance for my post surgeries, and I had the privilege of free medical care five days per week in addition to my infrequent visits to his office.

An inventory of my life, particularly during the years of 1973 to 1976, resembles a large puzzle in which so many people played a role. Shortly after my first surgery, one of my sisters from my adopted church family introduced me to a Jewish lawyer. This man's kindness and concern for my welfare resulted in my successful application for a work-permit visa at no monetary cost to me. In addition to his free legal services, I never once had to meet him at the immigration office. Instead, I would go to his office and he would drive me there. Reflecting on his act of benevolence, I am ashamed of how selfishly I acted during this period of my life. I never inquired about a bill—I simply accepted his service as free and providential. Although I was verbally thankful, I never even took the time to mail a thank you card.

The only explanation I have is the fact that I had not really matured with age. Although I had an independent mindset from childhood, I was emotionally impaired from the eight years of trauma caused by my mentally ill aunt. Life with my biological family did not encourage maturity because my sisters were very protective of me when I was at home. Perhaps they pitied me because of my facial impairment. Or, perhaps they believed my mark was a sign of physical illness. Whatever the source of their concern, I was deprived of age-appropriate functions and development.

On one hand, I was rebellious with assigned chores and felt that I should not have to do anything that anyone wanted me to do since I was not like everyone else. Of all the chores I was assigned, babysitting and cleaning were the only ones I enjoyed and chose to engage in. It had been my sisters who had picked up my slack.

On the other hand, I was jealous of my siblings because they were required to work in the garden or help with other adult-age responsibilities, and I could not. My doctors at the time did nothing to dispel my parent's prohibitions. For reasons I still did not understand, I was not allowed to do some of the fun things of childhood such as climbing trees. Now I see my resulting attitude as senseless, rebellious, and defiant.

Because of the kindness and healthy reception I received from the Rafetti family, I did not want to limit my contribution to just babysitting. I wanted to help them in any way necessary. This meant that I had to quickly learn all the responsibilities I neglected during my rebellious youth. By the mercy of a sovereign God, I succeeded to the effect of becoming a successful housekeeper. Dr. and Mrs. Rafetti appreciated me and spoke highly about my contributions to their family and to all their friends. My three years experiences with the Rafetti family allowed me to learn and to develop additional character traits and abilities that improved me.

Pastor Dennis Smith talks about how God uses storms in our lives to develop our faith and Christlike character in a devotional entitled "The Storms of Life" from his book *40 Days: Prayers and Devotions to Revive Your Experience with God, Book 2.* In this meaningful devotion, the story of Joseph is explained. Joseph was favored in a manner similar to the way I had been favored as a child. God wanted to use Joseph in a mighty way, so He allowed him to go through trials in order to build his character. Through adversity, God fulfilled Joseph's dreams. If Joseph had not become a slave and ended up in prison, how would he have become governor of Egypt, second only to Pharaoh? If the cupbearer had not waited to reveal Joseph to Pharaoh who would have interpreted Pharaoh's dream at his time of greatest need?

Joseph patiently waited and looked to God for deliverance throughout his trials. There may have been things in his life that happened to him for reasons that he did not understand, but he held to his faith. Even when it seemed as if God had forsaken him, he continued to trust in Him. Joseph endured the storms and was able to receive a great blessing because of it.

> God wanted to use Joseph in a mighty way, so He allowed him to go through trials in order to build his character.

Joseph's story is a lesson for us. When thrown into the severe storms of life, God wants us to know that we are in His hands, and that He has a divine purpose for us. Even the storms we enter by our own foolish hand can be used to teach us. Consider Psalm 107:17–20: "Fools, because of their rebellious way, and because of their iniquities, were afflicted. Their soul abhorred all kinds of food, and they drew near to the gates of death. Then they cried out to the Lord in their trouble; He saved them out of their distresses. He sent His Word and healed them, and delivered them from their destructions."

Through my surgeries, I learned new things that benefited me. It is important to remember that when we are facing life's storms, our God is capable of delivering us even if the storms were a result of our own foolishness. Even storms arising from our imprudence can work out for God's glory. Once I realized this, it gave me deeper insight into all the struggles and storms I experienced in my life. As never before, I perceived the storms as God's method of answering my constant prayer for better faith in Him. My mother had initiated this prayer for faith each night as she prayed over my face, and I continue to believe when everything in life has failed, faith in God prevails.

However, at the time of the storms that had only begun to rage in my life, I did not have such profound insight and trust in God's will. Therefore in 1976, when I was experiencing a time of rich blessings, I attributed this to be a natural result of my conversion and steadfast walk with God. This era of my Christian experience was also punctuated with my misconception of the foundation for a continuous, happy, fulfilled Christian life.

Because of the strong support systems, particularly the spiritual support of my church, I blossomed physically, emotionally, and spiritually despite this time of turbulence. All my needs were fulfilled in one form or another. This allowed me very little insight into the growing nature of salvation by faith, and it was almost thirty-five years before my encounter with Pastor Dennis Smith's inspired revelation. At this point, I had zero insight into seeing trials and difficulties as opportunities for growing faith and dependency on God.

In the midst of the trial of my medical regimen that had thus far only shown me the benefits of my conversion, my storms were about to increase. As the saying goes, "When it rains, it pours."

The first trouble came with the announcement that Dr. Rafetti had colon cancer, and it had come out of remission. The diagnosis was that it was aggressively progressing. At the time, the details were not available to me. I was simply informed that Dr. Rafetti would be seeing a doctor in New York and considering surgery because of some stomach problems. This would require Mrs. Rafetti's frequent overnight or day trips to New York. Mrs. Rafetti asked me if I would consider caring for their three children during their absence.

Even though I was unaware of the gravity of Dr. Rafetti's condition, I was more than willing to fill the role of housekeeper and babysitter for the three children. The experience was challenging to say the least. I found myself with a permanent three-year old shadow that was always demanding my attention, even while I was assisting the two school-age children to get up and ready for the school bus. This, too, was a learning experience in which I discovered that not compromising their bedtime was a helpful precursor for the early morning tasks. I traded some of my playfulness for firmness. My charges did not appreciate that I had suddenly traded my babysitting characteristics for motherly attributes, but it worked.

Out of necessity, I established my rules and implemented them without deviating from Mrs. Rafetti's own rules. For instance, I did not change bedtimes or the duration and types of television viewing the children could watch. However, I no longer accompanied the five-year-old while he watched his favorite puppet show after supper, because I needed that time to assist the youngest child with her bath and prepare her for bedtime. The five-year-old could then tell me about the show later. During this same time period, the oldest child was occupied with homework. Throughout all of this, each child was in competition to get more of my attention. I quickly had to learn that the command, "Rita, come here! Come quick!" did not mean there was an emergency, but was likely to be nothing more than the five-year-old wanting to share some observation about a cartoon that was playing or the three-year-old wanting me in the same room.

In my ignorance, I cherished the hopeful expectation of my doctor's soon recovery and the return to normalcy at the Rafetti's household. That hope was not realized. From the first doctor's appointments onward, the hospitalizations and follow-up visits continued. After his first surgery, Dr. Rafetti's frailty and weight loss became very noticeable. In fact, it was difficult to contain my sadness the day he returned home. When the front door opened and the weak man standing there resembled death more than life, I should have realized his illness was more serious than I initially perceived. Still I hoped.

Despite his condition, he still gave me the caring, connecting-smile and eye contact I enjoyed. He also inquired about my health and thanked me for being part of his family. I was heart-broken as I watched him slowly and painfully walk into the den after supper using all his effort. He could not pick up the youngest child as he usually did, but she was able to crawl into his lap once he sat. It was only a brief moment before he listened to his wife's suggestion and painfully made his way up the long flight of steps. Mrs. Rafetti tried to engage the children's attention away from what they had witnessed of their father while I returned to my chores in an attempt to normalize this rest of the day.

For weeks, Dr. Rafetti did not come down to breakfast or go to work. Most of his needs were met in his bed. His favorite breakfast at the time was my oatmeal. He liked it because I made it with milk instead of water, and I flavored it with vanilla and cinnamon. My love and appreciation for this man was so deep that I prepared it daily and willingly served him.

Since my workload had increased in an effort to relieve some of the burden from Dr. and Mrs. Rafetti, I had no time during the day to give in to feelings of self-pity about the situation. However, alone in my room, I frequently talked on the phone with my sister who prayed with me for strength. These prayers allowed me to physically and emotionally face the challenges of each new day despite any lack of sleep I had from my worry.

After a few weeks, the doctor regained enough strength to begin moving around more and was gradually able to go outside. Eventually, he resumed working a few hours per day. This exertion proved to be too much for him. Shortly after returning to work, his rapidly deteriorating health resulted in another long period of hospitalization.

This time I was better prepared for the household challenges that met me during Mrs. Rafetti's absence. I even began deftly fielding unending questions from the children.

"But why…?"

"I don't know," I would reply, "but don't forget to ask Mom when she returns."

When Mrs. Rafetti returned from New York, she informed me with relief that her mother-in-law had agreed to come stay with us for two weeks, when Mrs. Rafetti would soon return to her husband. Both of us felt this would lighten my burden, but Grandmother had burdens of her own with her son dying in the hospital. When she arrived, she hovered around the children. Unfortunately, they had grown used to their independence. They were also concerned about their father and had shorter tempers.

One day the situation came to a head. I heard the eldest child's screaming: "Leave me alone. Rita, get her out of my room! Get her out, Rita!" Usually, the eldest would go do her homework after supper and set out her clothes for the next day. She was not one to make a fuss. In fact, I seldom heard from her until it was bedtime, and she would sometimes call me in to her room for a visit or tell me what she wanted for breakfast the next day. I assumed that Grandmother had inadvertently disturbed her granddaughter's ritual.

When I arrived in the room I found an almost nine-year-old having a screaming tantrum and a perplexed senior citizen whose first words were, "What did I do?"

I quickly ushered the grandmother to the den and returned to console the child. I listened patiently to the explanation for her behavior and then gave her advice on how to better handle the situation should it occur in the future. As soon as the child's situation had been dealt with and the youngest was tucked in bed, I headed downstairs to talk with the grandmother.

Again, I patiently listened to the woman as she told me "I don't know what I did wrong. I was simply trying to be nice to her." I apologized for her granddaughter's behavior and reminded her that everyone had been going through a rough time with Dr. Rafetti's illness. In my ignorance and denial, I then shared my hope and prayer that her son would have a quick recovery and a return to his life as usual. I could not ignore the curious look on her face.

"You mean you don't know?" she asked.

"Don't know what?" I asked hesitatingly, not sure I wanted to hear her answer.

"My son is dying," she said sullenly. "He's been fighting this cancer a long time before you came. That's how he got so small. He was never a small man. After his first surgery years ago, he regained some of his weight and looked healthy. Now, the cancer is back, and he is so frail that his doctor here will not operate anymore. That's why he is going to New York. Oh, he is such a fighter, but it all seems hopeless now."

Inside I was devastated. I wanted to yell, "Shut-up! Don't tell me anymore!" Instead, I responded more calmly, "I am so sorry. I had no idea it was cancer. However, our God is able, so let's not give up on him."

Looking back on this experience, I see, again, an exaggeration of needless emotional pain because of my immature faith. However, I cannot be too hard on myself. My new birth excitement was enduring and intense. I had the support of Martha, my elders, other church families, and an active prayer and witnessing life. I also relied on providential intervention outside of the church to get me through my days. These blessings left me oblivious to the attacks of the enemy in his effort to rob me of my faith. I was an inexperienced soldier in Christ's army.

In addition, I had not yet learned from so many mature believers who triumphed in their dismal life circumstances by faith and fortitude. Yet, despite my weak faith, the Lord kept me. I can see today that what the devil meant for bad, the Lord turned to good. When encountering stormy days, I look back on the past. Remembering that God kept me, in spite of who I was, provides me with the courage for more trusting faith.

Chapter 15

A Journey Too Short

Our first notice that something was wrong came in the form of a letter from Mom telling us of our father's hernia surgery. We were concerned because this was his second hernia surgery, but we knew that nothing could be that serious about a re-occurring hernia. However, Martha and I felt much better after praying about the situation.

A second letter arrived almost one year later, informing us of Father's third surgery. Mom shared that it was for stomach problems, but gave us no more details. Perhaps in an effort to cheer us, she included a small photo of Father standing a long way from the camera. The picture was slightly concerning because Father had lost a significant amount of weight, but Mom's comments indicated he was recovering quickly.

In the next three months, we received no more worrying news from home, so we assumed that all was well. Whether this was due to some deception by my father's doctors, which would not surprise me considering the medical trend of that era of not disclosing information, or whether it was due to Mom's denial, we were deceived.

During this time, Martha had decided to return to Canada to resume her pursuit of a nursing career. Also, despite promising my father I would return home and help build a new house for our family after three years, I had decided to remain in the United States until my medical regimen was complete. Mrs. Stein was distressed over Martha's decision, so Martha recommended that she hire her best friend, Latisha in her stead; she would be my new roommate. Latisha had been in an abusive marriage and welcomed the offer to leave St. Lucia.

It was during the excitement of her arrival and our unending talk about home that we learned the truth of our father's condition. One of my father's nurses was friends with Latisha and Martha. She had informed Latisha that my father had the advanced stages of colon cancer. He could not have any more surgeries for his condition and had not been given much longer to live.

"I am shocked that you don't know," Latisha said as we stared at her blankly.

At this point, I was devastated. Although I had planned to return after three years, I had not finished my facial treatments, earned a secretarial degree, or taken any music classes. These were all things I hoped to accomplish while in the United States. Then I could return home, help my father build a new house, take a job that would lead toward social work, and perhaps pursue a secondary career as a singer. Not only had I not achieved these dreams, but I was faced with a decision to stay and support Dr. Rafetti, whom I loved as a father figure and as my doctor, or support my father as he battled the same disease at home.

I realized now that three years was too short a time to achieve all my goals. I may have been able to achieve my medical dreams, but when Dr. Rafetti fell ill, I refused to see the new plastic surgeon that he recommended. I believed that the new surgeon would be inferior not on a basis of his knowledge or skills but merely because he was not Dr. Rafetti, who I knew was assigned my case by Providence. I did not have faith that just as God worked through Dr. Rafetti, so He could also work through another doctor. It did not help that I had yet to succeed in praying my doctor back to health. My plans had been put on hold and now the time was up.

After careful consideration, I decided to go home to be with my biological father. The flight home was as short as my time in America seemed. It was not time enough to sort through all the emotions that raged within me. I was returning with nothing to show for my efforts. Even my suitcase had not been packed with fancy clothing and American souvenirs. Instead it carried mainly anti-cancer health foods and herbs meant to help my father in the recovery I was convinced he would make.

> I did not have faith that just as God worked through Dr. Rafetti, so He could also work through another doctor.

I always found the high altitude comforting. The realities of my life seemed less worrisome so high in the sky. I could have drifted forever, and the pilot's announcement of my final destination came much too soon.

I stepped off the plane and was pleased to discover that little had changed. The warm tropical breeze hit my face and the distasteful shout of "Taxi for you!" filled the air.

My return was planned as a surprise, so there were no familiar faces at the airport to welcome me. Sadly, I signaled the least aggressive driver, and he picked up my suitcase and gracefully escorted me to his taxi.

On any other day, I would have welcomed my driver's effort for friendly conversation. Instead, I reluctantly briefed him about my family, my time in America, and my premature return home because of my father's illness. He expressed his sorrow and concern, but I only wanted to change the subject, so I asked about his family. His world seemed much more interesting than mine.

I listened to his story as I watched him skillfully maneuver around the frequent curves that punctuated the steep, narrow road. He was familiar with Bardinee, my destination, so I only had to inform him of my stop at the top of a hill, next to a downhill path.

The stop came much too soon. If he was eager to return to another business of the day, he was successful at concealing it. We both said, "Thank you," and, "It was nice talking with you," repeatedly, and he promised to pray for my father.

On such a small island, news travels very quickly. To my surprise, a family friend who sighted me from a distance at some point of my journey home thought it necessary to inform my family of my arrival.

"I told her I was not surprised; I had been expecting you," said my mom. I, however, was greatly surprised by the skeleton of a man sitting folded over as if always ready to hug his constantly painful stomach. His facial expression lightened briefly as I approached him. His answers to my questions about his health and his doctor's orders were brief and evasive. I soon realized that he was not interested in discussing his condition, and neither was I. It was then that I tried another approach: I began cheerfully sharing my experience in America. That subject posed less discomfort until I thought of my doctor's health condition—I feared that if Father knew of Dr. Rafetti's terminal cancer it would rob him of his will to live. I abruptly changed the subject, and was grateful that he did not probe me about it.

The following days and nights were torture. I have heard that "Courage is the ability to separate from the familiar, or it is the will to persevere in spite of one's fear." When I look back on the ninety days I spent with my father during his illness, I know it took nothing less than courage to stay.

Everyone was carrying out his or her duties as expected, but the silent message of Father's pending death and our gloom were always present. The frequent inquiries and responses of those walking by did not help. It was hard to hear their promises of prayer on our behalf, but no more wishes that my father would be well soon. One could tell by looking at these passersby that they all missed my father's laughter and jokes, but I was too preoccupied with my own needs to notice they cared.

I committed all my tie and energy to caring for my father, and endeavored to meet his every need, particularly his nutrition. I accompanied him to several doctor's visits and asked many questions only to be ignored or to receive unrelated answers. Perhaps this could be attributed to the fact that I had become accustomed to being an active part of my own care, or perhaps the doctors felt I was not asking them the right questions. The latter may be especially true since all my questions were singularly focused on what more could be done for him.

Those were the last words I spoke to my father.

I ignored repeated invitations to visit with relatives and old friends. I wanted to be in my father's presence continually, as though willing him to live would keep him alive. On one occasion, when Mother finally convinced me to take a break, I did so just to appease her. I returned much sooner than she would have expected, because I feared that death would have an opportunity to steal Father in my absence.

Despite my reluctance to leave my father, I had to say goodbye. A letter from Mrs. Rafetti had reminded me of my incomplete goals and my need to return to the United States. I felt it was time to go back and finish what I started.

Father had been hospitalized for several days and was very weak. However, I leaned over the hospital bedrail to whisper goodbye and tell him I hoped he would be well soon, denying the obvious truth of his condition. Then I asked if he would like to send his greetings to Martha.

"Give her my best," he said, "but tell her I will not be here when she returns."

"Don't you dare say that to me!" I exclaimed. "I have never heard you tell a lie before, so why would you do it now?"

Those were the last words I spoke to my father. I should have told him how much I loved and appreciated him. I should have shared with him the love of God, and the blessed hope of the resurrection. I should have told him how this message of hope is effective for all who repent of their sins and are justified by faith by the blood of Christ Jesus.

Instead of sharing my faith, I called my father a liar. It is no wonder this experience haunted my memory for a very long time. I wish I knew then, that these adversities would later help to shape my life of faith.

When I now think about my life's trials and how poorly I dealt with them, I like to ponder the lyrics of the song "Blessings" by Laura Story.

In 1976, I had not heard these lyrics. I also had not read the words of Pastor Dennis Smith or any of the other contemporary writers of faith who underscore the positive outcomes of adversities. I am thankful, though, that my budding faith was enough to help me look to God for answers. I am also glad I can honestly say that I was never tempted to relinquish faith in God. Instead, the worse adversities left me praying for more faith. At the time, I did not correlate more trials with increased faith.

Chapter 16

New Beginnings

Some people say they no longer pray for faith because more trials seem to come instead. I cannot completely relate to this statement because it seems that whether or not I pray for faith, my trials are inevitable. I have learned from my experiences that a trusting faith is not possible unless I have been through trials to put it to practice.

My first experiences with faith came when my mom would say bedtime prayers with me. As we finished, she would draw a cross on my deformed face. Each morning, I would get up to check the mirror only to find there had been no miraculous healing in the night. Still, we continued to pray and trust God. We had no other choice because the result of my second surgery was more devastating than the first.

Although she did not verbalize it, I think by this time Mom had also lost faith in the doctors. The only option remaining to us was a total dependence on God. When I boarded the plane in September to return to the United States, I was again depending on Him.

My return flight to America was much less overwhelming than my flight to St. Lucia had been. Martha had returned to Ottawa almost a year before. I had planned to visit her for a week, which would offer a much-needed break from the cancer that had surrounded me for a long time.

I was looking forward to meeting Martha's roommate, Hyacinth, of whom Martha spoke highly. The excitement of visiting their church and meeting new people kept my outlook pleasant.

By the time I arrived I began to break through my denial about our father. I felt compelled to tell Martha the truth of his condition and his goodbye message to her.

I constantly found myself asking, "Why, Lord?" In the absence of an explicit answer to this question, I found much comfort in the reminder that God knows best. I also found comfort in knowing Martha and I had prayerfully and painstakingly overcame many challenges throughout our Christian walk. I anticipated we would use the same weapon to fight against our father's illness.

To my dismay, Martha had already accepted Father's death as inevitable, outside of a miracle. Still unwilling to let go, I judged her acceptance as being too quick. However, because of the time I spent in thought during my travels, I was able to realize that she was right. From that time on, our prayers for Father always ended with, "God's will be done."

We had a wonderful time visiting during that week. In fact, it was much more enjoyable than I anticipated. I seemed to fit right in with Martha's friends, and they accepted me. The kind, caring, humorous Hyacinth became a cherished new friend as well. Martha and Hyacinth were so much alike, and their sisterly relationship was evident.

At first I was tempted to accept the invitation to stay another week. It was a beautiful area accentuated by the magical colors of fall, clean-fresh air, clean streets, and a friendly culture. Human courtesy, dignity, and community surrounded me. We spent most of the day shopping and sight seeing, dressed in clothing appropriate for early fall. Suddenly, there was a piercing wind and cooler temperatures, and I found myself shivering. It was so cold that we decided to call an end to our activities for the day, and I thought that perhaps I should leave as planned after all.

"It's time to return to America, where the seasons are defined not just by name but also by temperature," I laughed. "I thank you all for being so nice, but I am ready to go home."

At the time, I merely used the term "home" in reference to my temporary living arrangements. I was sure I would only be there another three years until I accomplished my goals. I had no idea how wrong this assumption was.

My return to America was like another new beginning. Despite my positive attitude and adequate support, many changes had occurred during my absence that affected my life. First I had to adjust to the fact that Dr. Rafetti had passed away. I also learned that Mrs. Rafetti could only afford my housekeeping services two days per week. Thankfully, four of her friends considered my one-day per week housekeeping service. I had decided to only work Monday through Friday so finding a way to fit six days of housekeeping into five days was tricky. They solved the problem for me when two of the ladies were generous enough to split one of the workdays. I went to one household in the morning and the other in the afternoon.

> I was sure I would only be there another three years until I accomplished my goals. I had no idea how wrong this assumption was.

Another challenge that arose involved finding my own place to live. I could not live with Mrs. Rafetti because of the position, and my old roommate could not finance our large home while I was away, so she had relocated to a smaller apartment that was better suited to her and her son. When I first arrived, they were kind enough to share this space with me, but I knew staying too long would impose on their comfort and be very inconsiderate. This drove me to move on and find a better place for myself.

While I was trying to organize my new life again, I continually prayed for my father. I opened each new letter with fear that it would inform me of his death. However, the news did not come by post. One day Martha called, and I just knew that our father had died. I could tell from the sound of her voice. She shared with me that Father had died on December 4, 1976.

No matter what happens, I always try to live each day to its fullest. However, on this day, the news of my father's death turned my whole world upside down. When I think back to that time, I see a prolonged period when the enemy of my soul could have seized opportunity after opportunity to permanently sever my relationship with God.

Although I was vexed with God, He did not leave me in my confused state. Instead, He provided ample indication of his love and mercy. He met me where I was and carried me to where I needed to be.

As always, I received full support from my church family. During this time of utter sorrow, I remember talking on the phone with Pastor Keith Dennis. After chatting and praying with me, he asked if I was planning to attend a wedding that would take place at the church in two weeks.

"I'm sorry," I responded. "I don't really feel up to it."

He was very determined not to accept my "no" for an answer and kept prodding me to come.

"I don't have any thing to wear," I finally told him. "And I'm broke."

"Just be in church on Sabbath," he replied to my surprise, "and we will take care of that."

I did go to church that Sabbath, but not just because of the pastor's promise. I went because of God's prompting. When I was leaving after the service, the pastor wore his broadest smile and directed me to the head elder. The elder slipped an envelope into my hand.

As I opened the envelope moments later, I was thrilled with what I saw. It was enough money to buy a beautiful gown and matching shoes. There is something about a new outfit and fellowship with other believers that can take away a bit of grief.

Once they discovered I needed a place of my own, one of the members of our church's early-morning prayer group, Brother Campbell, took the responsibility of assisting me with relocating. Several church families frequently invited me to their homes and helped to reduce the amount of time I was alone.

God's mercy and love was also apparent with my friends and employers outside of church. In four of the homes where I worked, I performed my light housekeeping duties while the children were in school and the parents at work. Although all of my employers seemed concerned with overworking me, one in particular provided me with a period of relaxation. During my double half-day, the morning job consisted of a visit with Mrs. Manix. She worked for a stockbroker and her husband owned a garage. Their only daughter was away at college.

Mrs. Manix was warm, caring, and intelligent. She would meet me at the door, dressed and ready for work, and would invite me to join her at the table. While we visited for the next hour, we enjoyed some of her favorite Jewish pastries. She knew I did not drink coffee, so she provided me with herbal tea. After answering many of her questions, I usually tried to end the socializing and begin work.

"So, what's on the to-do list today?" I asked, pushing away from the table.

"Nothing much," Mrs. Manix would reply, motioning me back to my sit.

Eventually, she would decide that our interlude was finished. Then we would clean up our dishes and she would remind me that there was a bag of poultry or meat for me in the freezer. She also left a bag of Jewish baked goods on the table for me, along with much more money than I felt was deserved for a half-day's work.

After that, she walked me downstairs to the laundry room where clean garments needed to be folded or ironed. The rest of her house was spotless, and I never had to lift a finger to do any of it.

"Thank you for coming. I so enjoy talking with you." She would say as she went to her office.

All of the support I received was very helpful as I grieved for my father, but I still developed digestive problems. After eating, I experienced extreme heartburn that made me hesitant to eat even when I was extremely hungry. I learned that worry, fear, and a lack of faith can lead to both emotional and physical issues. As Pastor Adrian Rogers says, "The door of opportunity swings on the hinges of opposition."

With limited finances and no medical insurance, a visit to the doctor was not possible. Instead, I resorted to natural remedies. I found the book, *Back to Eden* by Jethro Kloss, and implemented its regimen for total body cleansing and blood purifying. The key features described in the book included a two-week diet of fresh fruits, raw vegetables (particularly cabbage), fresh vegetable and fruit juices, and herbal cleansing teas (particularly Golden Seal, Red Clover, and White Clover). The exclusions included meats and refined foods (particularly white sugar and white flour products).

For the first few days of this diet, I underwent some discomfort (hunger, weakness, and lightheadedness). However, the remaining days brought remarkable internal and external results. When I arrived at Mrs. Rafetti's four days after beginning the diet, she greeted me with excitement.

"The door of opportunity swings on the hinges of opposition."

"Rita, what have you been doing? Your skin is glowing with health! You've lost significant weight in a short time—yet you look healthy."

"I was having problems with my stomach, so I am trying a new diet," I replied, explaining the book I had found.

"But I have heard a diet of constant roughage can cause digestive problems," Mrs. Rafetti said, amazed.

"I do not know why this one is working for me, but it is," I responded.

In less than one week, my digestive problems ended. This experience was my first conviction of the health benefits of a meatless diet. At one point, I almost converted to vegetarianism, but my love of chicken prevailed.

During this time of new beginnings, I was given the opportunity to learn healthier, more productive ways of thinking. Though the summer of 1976 was devastating for me, autumn brought new hope, along with glorious color and beauty.

"What are your plans for the future, Rita?" Mrs. Rafetti inquired one day.

"I'm saving toward classes right now so I can obtain a high school diploma," I replied without hesitation. "Once I have that, I will pursue a secretarial degree. I intend to accomplish this within the next two years. During the third year, I will take some music classes. By the end of 1979, I plan to go back to St. Lucia and work for the government as a secretary."

"You don't need to take classes to get a GED with your level of intelligence," replied Mrs. Rafetti. "All you need to do is get the book, review, and apply for the exam. However, I am concerned about your plans for a secretarial career. Considering your ability for neatness and structure, I have no doubt you could be a good secretary, but I think you would be wasting your time. I think your talents lie in providing services for special needs children."

The first part of Mrs. Rafetti's response was gratifying, but I viewed the rest of her statement as almost an insult. I did not realize until decades later that I equated her response with the one I was given years before by the interviewer who told me I was intelligent and capable, but would never be hired as a secretary because of my face. My determination to prove this man wrong motivated me to continue pursuing my goals regardless of the wisdom and advice of others.

Looking forward, I see how my failure to deal with my emotions and to forgive resulted in a subconscious desire to prove this interviewer a liar. Without realizing it, I had allowed this man to control me for approximately ten years. Many years of difficult and discouraging experiences could have been significantly lessened had I heeded Mrs. Rafetti's warning. However, I gave no thought to her observation about wasting my time as a secretary. I thought she, too, was saying I could not be a secretary because of my face. I became determined to prove her wrong as well. I did listen to her suggestion about my GED. Mrs. Rafetti even purchased the book for me so I could prepare. In a matter of weeks, I obtained a GED.

The following year, I was hired by the school system through a temporary agency as a receptionist. Another short-term receptionist and secretarial position soon followed with a large insurance company.

This new job was overwhelming, not because of the responsibilities, but because of the emotional stress from my unresolved issues. It was difficult to hide the tears from the emotions that I had while performing my duties. I frequently fled to the restroom, crying in anger and frustration. Instead of appreciating the fact that I had made it to a temporary position as a secretary, I focused on how close I was to being a secretary without achieving the actual goal.

After battling with this problem for weeks, I called Martha. My kind sister reminded me of my bravery and accomplishments, and assured me of her prayers. That intervention worked. The months ahead found me enjoying and appreciating the reality of being so close to my goal. I envisioned a permanent position with this company as a full time secretary, and it almost happened.

Early in 1978, my supervisor informed me about an opening for a clerk in the underwriter's department. The pay was average, but the benefits were excellent. After my first year of employment, the company would pay for my continuing education in any field that could benefit them. If I stuck to my plan to return to St. Lucia in 1979, I would not be able to take part in this offer.

In the end, I accepted the offer. This decision turned out to be very good. In addition to liking my job, I liked my coworkers very much. I was the only dark-skinned employee in my department, but those I worked with were very supportive.

One of my favorite memories of working there was the morning when I found my desk covered in cupcakes. To this day, I have no idea who planned this birthday surprise or how it got to my desk. I thought I was the first one to arrive at the office that day, but the cupcakes were there before me.

Despite the pleasure I found in my job and my continued desire for a secretarial degree, I experienced another major change during this time that caused me to reevaluate my plans once more.

At church, I felt it was my duty to make everyone feel as welcome as I had felt. There was a man named Joseph who tended to hang on the edge of the group and frequently wore an expression that said he would rather be left alone. I wanted to include him in our circle of love and friendship, so I made an effort to sit next to him and become acquainted. When I took the initiative to converse with him, I always found him very likable.

After several months, he asked me to accompany him to our church's fall social event, which allowed us an opportunity to get personally acquainted. To my surprise, Joseph's childhood dilemmas made mine look like a picnic.

Joseph was born in Hartwell, Georgia, in 1942. I was shocked to hear the horror stories that he and his family experienced. Even though slavery had been abolished during the Civil War, the racism and bigotry of those residing in the South had not magically disappeared. Families would labor all year for the owners of plantations under the sharecropper system and then pay most or all of it to the owner after the harvest. If the family ran out of funds, they would have to borrow it in a manner similar to coal miners and their scrip. It was not uncommon to discover that after a year of hard labor they merely "came out even." There were no good jobs for those who had any slave ancestry, and poverty was rampart. Children as young as six were put to work in the fields helping to pay the way of the family, or they had to stay home alone and watch younger siblings. Even when they could save up enough money to pay the poll tax and vote for a better government to support them, their votes were not counted.

When Joseph was eight, he found a firecracker and decided to light it. He tossed it and it happened to land in a white man's yard. The firecracker did no damage, but the man had Joseph arrested and thrown in jail with drunks. It took his family the entire day to raise enough money to free him.

As Joseph relayed this injustice, a teardrop rolled out of my eye and onto my cheek. When he noticed, he told me that was enough because he would not have me crying over his past.

After that, we began getting to know each other better. Joseph told me how he had watched the landowners to learn useful skills that allowed him to earn an adult wage even as a teenager, but he still had to submit to unspoken, humiliating rules. For example, if a white woman happened to be walking toward them, they would need to step off the sidewalk and let her go through. This treatment is what made him leave his home state and seek a better life in the Northeast.

During our frequent time together over the following months, we discussed each other's interests and discovered that we had much in common when it came to spirituality, goals, and aspirations. We both wanted to work hard and retire early so we could spend time in the mission fields during our early senior years.

I do not know when our relationship transformed from platonic to romantic, but before long, the focus of our lives shifted to us as a couple. Joseph wanted to own a machine shop, so we considered how my role as secretary could help the family business. At first I thought the option of secretary in that situation would be condescending. My goal was to be an executive secretary in a functioning business. Since I wanted to prove that I could be hired as a secretary despite my face, it took a long time before I could accept that working anywhere as a secretary was a worthy accomplishment.

Chapter 17

His Will or Mine?

November 25, 1979, was one of the happiest days of my life. Every young woman dreams of walking down the aisle in a wedding gown. I had none of my biological family to help me, but my church family helped me greatly. One of our church members, Sister Bailey, assumed the responsibility of designing and sewing the bridesmaids' gowns. She also baked the wedding cake and assisted in other areas. I welcomed her suggestions and considered her contributions a great blessing. I was exhausted from all the work, but it was well worth it.

With everything going my way, I knew I was doing God's will, and no one could convince me otherwise. I thought to myself, *I love the Lord, and so does my new husband. We are starting out with very little, but with God on our side, the future looks bright.*

One week after our wedding, we traveled to Hartwell, Georgia. Before we left, Joseph assured me the climate there was almost as tropical as St. Lucia's climate. Based on this expectation, I left all my winter clothes behind, except for a coat Martha had given me.

My first winter in Hartwell seemed almost as cold as winter in Connecticut. Because of our limited finances and difficulty finding jobs, we could not afford extra clothing. I was grateful for my one coat, which I wore that entire winter. Although I found it difficult, I did eventually forgive Joseph's misguided advice because he had never actually been to a tropical island.

Our honeymoon was short lived, and we soon engaged in intense job searching. We did not foresee employment hardships since Joseph was experienced with tool and die casting and I had clerical experience. Time soon proved us wrong. Joseph assured me that racism in the area was not what it once was, but I frequently returned to follow-up on applications I had submitted in person, only to find they were missing and had not been received. I am not sure if the prejudice I experienced was due to racism, my accent, or my deformed face. Perhaps it was a combination of all these, but our job searching efforts proved futile.

After six months of unemployment, our future began to look bleak. In order to save enough money for the family business we desired to own, we needed jobs. We would also need our dream business to succeed quickly so that we could retire early and work in the mission field. All our hopes rested upon finding employment.

Prior to our move, we felt that we had both the determination and drive to pursue these goals. We also trusted that Jehovah, the all-powerful God, had the same goals for our life and would help us achieve them. We knew He would bless because we agreed to always give Him first place in our lives, including our marriage.

Looking back, I can see our perception was greatly in error. First, we were deceiving ourselves in thinking that we were putting God first. If we had been putting God first, we would have consulted with God and asked Him to show us His will in our lives. We also would have placed our missionary endeavor at the beginning of our lives together, not at the end. Finally, we approached our goals with the attitude that God owed us something for our dedication to Him instead of realizing that we owed Him our lives because of what He has done for us.

When it came to searching for a job, I know my husband faced even greater challenges than I did. There were times during our long months of seeking employment that Joseph would go missing. I would find him hidden away someplace, crying. Even when he took the first job that was offered to him, I would still find him hiding this way. This was partly because he was not hired as a skilled tool and die maker, but as a lower-level machinist. To make matters worse, he received $6.50 per hour and would arrive home covered in Georgia's red clay, which told me that he was mainly performing the work of a common laborer. However, Joseph never said a word about it.

My self-esteem dropped with each passing day that I could not find a job. Joseph continued to look for work and ended up with another machinist job in Anderson, South Carolina. He would be receiving a better wage and perform work that was closer to his expertise.

Anderson was a large city, so we decided to relocate. I felt that my opportunities for finding a clerical job would be better. In my mind, if I could just get my foot in the door with any employer, the rest would be history. God had opened many doors in my past, so I had no reason to think this would not continue.

Once we settled into Anderson's Fairview Gardens Apartments, I began my job search once more. In Hartwell we had one vehicle, and that had not caused much of a problem with my job search. However, when Joseph took the car to his 7:00–3:30 job five days a week, I was without transportation in a much bigger city. This did not deter me. I made my appointment with the Equal Employment Opportunity Commission and a few days later received notice of an opportunity that I saw as providential.

I went to interview to be a secretary in the magistrate's office. I was confident in my ability to meet the minimum test of 35 words per minute with no more than five errors. There was little apprehension on my part during the interview.

"We have several applicants," the interviewer concluded, "but you will hear from us as whether or not you are considered for the position."

When I returned home, I retained my confidence about the job. However, Joseph did not feel comfortable with me walking such a long way everyday in the downtown area.

"But this will be the last time," I promised.

Again, my mind saw the future as sure. Once I got the job, I could ride with Joseph on my way to work, and later we would be able to purchase a second vehicle.

For two weeks I checked the mail, anticipating a letter filled with the good news of my employment. Nothing arrived for me. Instead, a letter arrived that was addressed to Joseph from a Greenville company.

Greenville, South Carolina, was 45 miles away from Anderson and the company was offering Joseph a job there. We never considered the thought of commuting. Instead we packed our things and moved again.

Within days after our relocation to Greenville, I received a letter from the magistrate's office requesting that I report to work the following week. Since my commuting would have been out of the question with only one vehicle, I had to decline the position. I cried the entire time I wrote the letter, but I found solace in the fact that Greenville was an even bigger city than Anderson and therefore must have more opportunities. A bigger city meant a ten-mile roundtrip walk to the unemployment office, and Joseph continued to worry for my safety.

We had not lived in Greenville long when we experienced another difficult situation. We were traveling to our church in Anderson one Sabbath when a motorist, whose focus was not on his driving, smashed into our vehicle. Joseph retained a severe back injury and the doctor prescribed several days of rest for him to recuperate. Joseph's employer disagreed with the doctor's prognosis and insisted that he return to light-duty work. This was the tool and die job my husband had longed to do, so he returned to work to retain his employment. However, it was not long before his boss fired him anyway. Ironically, Joseph found his next job back in Anderson County, and we have lived there ever since.

One would think that all the trouble I was having with finding secretarial employment would have made me realize that I was pursuing it relentlessly to exact revenge on a person whom I would never meet again. Without recognizing this destructive force in my life, I continued my search.

Between 1981 and 1990, I had many disappointing experiences but refused to attempt another line of work. For example, I applied to a state program and assumed employment was based on meeting objective criteria. Applicants were required to achieve a relatively low passing grade in typing, basic math, and English. Once an applicant met these requirements, they were listed for jobs throughout the state. I submitted my application, went in for the interview, and aced the simple exam. I was very comfortable with my chances of obtaining employment, but I never got another call.

The applications for these positions were terminated annually. Any applicant who wanted to remain active had to resubmit their application and retake the exam each year. Four years later, I had still not received a job, but the interviewers and directors knew me in the office. One day, as I walked in to retake the exam, the interviewer looked me straight in the eye.

"I do not understand why you haven't been hired," she said. "Year after year you come, and you past your tests, including the typing tests that most people take two or three times. I just don't understand it."

"Neither do I," I responded.

Several days later, I ran into two ladies talking about their secretarial positions in this program. I was fascinated that these women had made it into a position I wanted.

"Well, I have been working as a secretary for more than two years, but I never passed my typing test," one said.

"But how were you able to do that?" I asked, baffled at this news.

"Because I knew somebody," she replied.

At this point, I refused to apply to the state program any longer. Sadly, I did not rule out all secretarial positions. I saw the closed door to the state secretarial position and believed like Maria von Trapp that God must have opened a window to another secretarial position somewhere.

Joseph was having his own problems at his job. He had lost two more high paying positions since our return, and racism was probably involved in both cases.

At the first job, Joseph's supervisor told every employee in the tool room to clean their own areas at the end of the workday. One worker swept, but then piled all his garbage in the corner and left. The supervisor arrived on the scene and told Joseph, who was still cleaning his area, to clean up the mess his coworker left as well. Of course, as you my have guessed, Joseph did not comply with this command, and he came home with his pink slip that day.

We tried to report the employer to the Equal Employment Opportunity Commission. To our surprise, they simply told us, "Nothing can be done based on South Carolina law. According to the law, 'You can get fired for a good reason, a bad reason, or no reason at all.'"

My only hope is that this law has been changed since 1986 when we were informed about it.

Joseph continued to have back problems, and he lost his second job because of this impairment. He had been out on sick leave after back surgery and his employer insisted he return to work once more. The employer promised he would only be put on light duty, but the first day ended up in horror. Joseph returned home dragging his feet, one after the other, as if every step was a painful effort. I had to untie his shoes and pull them off after he finally made it to the bed. It was then that I learned his 'light-duty' work included that he carry his own heavy steel to perform his machine operations. He was also forbidden to sit while the cycle was in operation. In other words, in addition to toting more weight than he should have, he had been forced to stand on a cement floor all day only a few weeks after back surgery.

The situation at this job had not been good before the surgery. Joseph had been experiencing chronic back and leg pain for a long time. One day he had passed two talking coworkers in an effort to clock out and had received a kick in the rear for it. When he reported the incident, it resulted in a one-week suspension for the perpetrator.

Joseph's coworkers and supervisors showed him nothing but contempt, so when he was finally laid off a few weeks after his painful return from back surgery, he looked at it as an opportunity rather than a setback. In 1987 he decided it was time to purchase his own machine shop.

By this time, I was more than halfway through a two-year program to receive an associate's degree in business at Tri-County Technical College. A friend of mine who was a secretary informed me that there was a position opening with her employer, and she managed to arrange an interview for me. The interviewer was very supportive.

"With your level of experience and your intelligence you shouldn't be unemployed," she said. "However, I see what could be working against you. You have been out of the clerical field for years. Your application is screened along with others who are in the field but are looking for better pay and better benefits. Many applications we receive are similar to yours, but we really need someone with knowledge of medical terminology. If you would consider completing a three-month course in medical terminology, it would allow you an advantage over your competitors. In fact, I can guarantee you the position you want if you complete this training."

Ms. Johnson* proceeded to discuss the benefits, salary, and responsibilities with me.

Of course, I not only considered the offer, I accepted it readily. It was not until after agreeing that I discovered the required class was not available through any educational institutions in Anderson. It was offered at Greenville Technical College, which was an approximately seventy-minute drive roundtrip. In my mind, this was a small price to pay for making my dream come true. If at the time I had known it would lead to the accident that almost took my life, I probably still would have felt the price was worth it. I was so focused on my goal at this point in my life that I did not perceive the danger to not only my physical life but also my spiritual life.

The car accident I was in on July 21, 1987, not only robbed me of another secretarial employment opportunity—it nearly ended the life I had built, including my hopes, my ambitions, my values and morals, my relationships with God, my husband, and my family. I am referring to all that fabric of my persona—without which I could be just existing instead of living—all of this could have been extinct as a vapor had God not intervened.

I left Greenville Technical College later than usual that day, and was running late for another secretarial job interview. The day before, we had hurriedly vacated our old address in order to provide living space for our church's Bible worker and her family. With such a heavy schedule, I was very tired and sleep deprived.

The seatbelt law was new in our state and I often forgot to comply. A careless driver pulled out of an intersection, and I tried to maneuver to keep from rear-ending him. Unfortunately, I lost control of my car, which turned over three times and ended upside down. My entire body was folded into a ball and neatly tucked under the steering wheel.

The accident could have easily taken my life, but it was evident that God had another purpose for me. However, I did sustain three fractured vertebra, three broken ribs, and a broken collar bone. My right arm was almost severed in two, and though not detectable at first, my brain injury was worst of all.

It took the rescue squad a long time to remove my limp, unconscious body from the vehicle. A newspaper article later reported that the stretcher carrying my body was not completely out when the vehicle caught fire. Only God's sustaining hand kept me from the flames.

Although I lost two weeks of my life to amnesia, I am thankful that my brain injury was not as devastating as it could have been. Shortly before the accident, I heard the story of a teenage girl, who suffered a traumatic brain injury (TBI) after a terrible injury. Unfortunately, her TBI was so severe that her memory was completely wiped out and she had to relearn everything about her life. I later realized I could have suffered the same result.

---

*   Name has been changed

Interestingly, no one suspected my brain injury at first. Everyone except Joseph said I seemed completely normal. I did not allow anyone to feel sorry for me. Joseph first realized something was very wrong as he observed my actions in the emergency room. He told me later that the staff had a difficult time keeping me on the bed because I repeatedly insisted that I needed to go home.

"I was scared to death at the sight of your nearly severed arm," Joseph told me.

"I'm glad I don't have that memory," I replied.

My inability to remember Martha and her son's visit was the first indication that I had a memory blackout. A little more than two weeks into my hospital stay, I received a call from Martha.

"Why aren't you here?" I joked. "Your sister almost died and you didn't even show up."

"What do you mean?" she responded.

"Just what I said," I insisted.

Martha questioned me several more times, but my response was always the same.

"Are you serious?" she finally asked. "Don't you remember that Ricky and I visited you for two weeks? Don't you remember how I bathed you, and brushed and combed your hair?"

It was very painful to accept my blank memory, but Martha's revelation was only the first of many. In the days, weeks, and months afterward, I had numerous conversations with Joseph, friends, and family that went much the same way.

I only revealed my two-week memory loss to Joseph and Martha. I turned to my neurosurgeon in an attempt to understand and deal with what had happened.

"You have just been through a lot," he replied without actually explaining.

The three months I spent on my back had a positive effect on my spiritual life. I devoted time to reading God's Word and constant prayer. Normally, I would read the Bible in the morning and in the evening. The accident made me an avid, prayerful reader of not only the Bible but also my collection of other inspired books and periodicals. My friends increased my library with gifts of books primarily about Jesus' Second Coming. Some were nonfiction and others, including *Project Sunlight* by June Strong, were fictional but spiritually enriching.

I eventually spent so much time in prayer during this season that I felt like I had no more sins to confess. I am not sure if this was because I had become self-righteous, or if the Holy Spirit had left me and was no longer convicting me of my sin.

Sinless living remained my great concern for the next three months. Finally, I was blessed with the ability to leave my bed. During this time, my husband had administered all my personal needs. Although my biological family members were absent physically, they provided encouragement through phone calls and financial support. We were also blessed by the ministry of our church family, particularly our Married Couple's Club.

I was worried about all of the additional responsibilities Joseph had to take on. Besides meeting my personal needs and taking care of our housekeeping, he had just started his new business, The Machine Shop. From what I saw, he appeared to manage everything quite well. Once I was able to get out of bed and move around the house, I realized this was not actually the case. Our home was disheveled at best.

The most disheartening sight was that of my houseplants, including some beautiful ones I had received during my recovery.

During this time, I learned the joy of forgiveness. Shortly before the accident, I had been humiliated by a person I considered my best friend who had told a horrible lie about me. I carried that emotional pain with me during my early recovery. At the onset of my prayerful study and a closer relationship with God, I was able to see the enemy of my soul, the devil, working through human instruments to discourage me. Rather than allowing myself the luxury of a pity party, including such questions as, "Why me, Lord? How can this happen to me?" I instead asked myself, "Why not me? Look at what they did to Christ. Am I better than He is?" As a result, I resolved to pray not only for myself but also for my accuser and her believers.

Even after learning the joy of forgiveness, I did not realize that I still needed to forgive the interviewer from long ago in St. Lucia. It is very possible that I was too much in denial to hear the voice of the Holy Spirit regarding this matter. Despite the pain my focus on a secretarial career had already caused, it continued to be my goal. The only difference was that I rationalized my continued desire by justifying my need to work to help financially.

My doctor advised me to take things easy for the first year, so I could achieve the best possible recovery. However, approximately five months after resuming my household responsibilities, I felt like I was back to normal. I could not resist the urge to begin pursuing my goals once more. At the time, I equated this with living again. Now I see that I was merely giving in to what had become an obsession.

With any addiction comes denial, and denial inhibits judgment. This was definitely true in my situation. My impaired judgment resulted in an inability to connect my pursuit with the harm I caused to myself and to others. For instance, my decision to return to my Tri-County curriculum caused grave concerns for my husband and family members. They feared that I would be vulnerable to having more accidents.

Inebriated by my desire for triumph, I continued to ignore the many obvious warning signs of my condition. In fact, I decided I would make up for the lost time by taking more classes per semester. This was easier planned than done. I soon discovered that the accident had not only caused two weeks of memory loss, but I also had some long-term memory deficits. I had severe problems with my math and computer skills. I could not retrieve my previous knowledge in these areas.

Prior to the accident, I managed to maintain a B average. After the accident, one of my teachers even asked me what had happened to all my computer skills. I did not know the answer to her question. Before the accident, I was almost to the point of completing all my required coursework, and now I was performing both math and computer at a beginner level.

Despite yet another wall of difficulties, I did not give up on my goal. I pressed on, determined to work hard as always. As a result, I crammed my days full of work and study, depriving myself of sleep. One morning, as I was driving to school with teary eyes and a weary, scattered mind, I overlooked an oncoming school bus at a four-way intersection.

Thankfully, no one, including any of the children, was seriously injured. Later, the thought of traumatizing innocent children because of my persistent, self-destructive will made me realize the extent of my insensitivity. In addition to the guilt I carried with me, I also had to begin paying a higher price for auto insurance.

After all of this, I still stubbornly pursued my secretarial degree. My GPA decreased drastically, but I considered the semester a success because I did not fail.

The following semester proved to be even worse. My computer classes were finished, but I still needed my erased math skills. My struggles with secretarial accounting helped me realize the gravity of my memory deficits. In addition to my long-term memory loss, I also discovered problems with my short-term memory. I could not store or retrieve information effectively. Despite my fervent efforts of extensive study time, maximum tutoring, and every available opportunity for questionings with my professor, at best I hoped to achieve a C so I could just pass secretarial accounting. Then I was in yet another accident.

The scenario was just the same. I was staying up into the early hours of the morning to study, then getting up to drive to school. One morning, I was overcome by sleep on my way to school. Fortunately, I was wearing my seat belt. My vehicle skipped the embankment and turned halfway over, but I was able to crawl out, seemingly unharmed. I stood on the side of the road, wondering how I would get to my classes, not worrying how I would get my vehicle home.

Thankfully, a senior motorist stopped and offered help. After explaining the cause for the accident as reasonably as I could, she asked if she could call someone to assist me with a way home.

"That would be my husband," I said. "But I am more concerned about not missing my classes today than I am concerned about my vehicle or getting rest."

Against the woman's better judgment, I convinced her to take me to school.

I was a few minutes late but was thankful to arrive safely. I ignored my need to use the restroom and headed straight to my first class. After class, my reflection in the restroom mirror did not convince me I was blessed just to be alive. Yet all I could think of was getting to my next class.

Meanwhile, my husband and his friend were on their way to Clemson University to negotiate a business contract. They were traveling my usual route to Tri-County. Suddenly, Joseph's friend called attention to my car lying sideways with the driver's side wheels in the air. Stopping their car, they were glad that my body was nowhere to be found, but they were concerned by the thought that I could be either in the hospital or on my way to the hospital. My husband had to take hope in the fact that no one had called him with this news.

With nothing more left for them to do, they proceeded to attend to their business. Once that was finished, they returned with his truck and towed my car long before I called Joseph for a ride home. He did not sound surprised or overwhelmed.

Despite my determination to achieve my goal, I still failed secretarial accounting. I found comfort in the thought that God was not finished with me yet. Amidst so many near-death experiences, I was still alive.

The following year found me more humble and more confident. I believed that my faith was stronger, and I was experiencing a surge of wisdom and maturity. I ended my last semester and prepared for graduation, but was not overly excited by my accomplishment. Instead, when I received the degree in 1990 I once thought would be my passport to a worthy career, I asked myself the question, "Was this worth it?"

For the first time, the reality of what I had put myself through was brought into focus. Suddenly, I was convicted to consider my husband's need for assistance with the family business rather than quenching my thirst for professional achievement.

In the field of addiction, a good definition for "denial" is "don't even know I am lying." Looking back, I can see that even my shift of focus continued my denial. I considered my husband's suggestion for my help to pacify my guilt over the negative outcomes of my selfish pursuits. In addition, I was still able to use the secretarial position at my family business to prove that the interviewer in St. Lucia so long ago was a deceiver and a liar. My denial made it difficult to acknowledge the intensity of my impaired judgment.

Chapter 18

My Defining Moment

Operating our small business required constant hard work with very little pay. There were also many stressful challenges that we encountered when we were competing against large corporations. We were thankful for the intervention of the Small Business Administration (SBA). With their assistance, we survived five difficult years. In fact, our buffer and motivation through those years was our promised certification by SBA which would qualify us to bid on contracts set aside by the Department of Defense (DOD) for small businesses.

This certification required evidence of our ability to meet the DOD's specifications in both manufacturing and administration. We met these requirements even though they were very tedious and challenging. When the DOD representative stamped our final approval documentation at the end of the five-year evaluation, we believed we were well on our way to a successful business.

However, the system failed us drastically. As a small business with five years of near financial drought, we could not satisfy the financial requirements of the contracts without relying on our banker. On one hand, the banker required that we first obtain the contracts before he would lend us the money for the overhead expenses. On the other hand, the DOD required that we obtained the loan before they would release the contracts.

Competing against large companies with more than 50 employees was impossible. According to regulations, businesses with more than 50 employees were exempted from bidding opportunities on the contracts set aside for small business, but many of the larger corporations manipulated the system. They found ways to meet the criteria set up to exclude them. Because of these two obstacles, our anticipated success quickly turned to failure. Almost one year after meeting the criteria for bidding on DOD contracts, we closed the door to Optimal Tool and Machine.

By then, Joseph's medical condition relating to his chronic back and leg pain had progressed. In addition, his previously mentioned experiences of job discrimination and humiliation were poor motivation for rejoining the job market. On this basis, Joseph reluctantly applied for medical disability.

By then, I was too burned out to think about any success or accomplishments I made in my long, sought-after goal of executive secretary. I simply thought about my need to work for survival. Because my long-term experiences were clerically based, I had no other choice but to focus my search in that field. With a degree in business and secretarial science, I did not foresee any difficulties in obtaining a job in my field.

Once again, I faced familiar rollercoaster of job searching. I finally enlisted with a temporary service agency in hopes of eventually finding a permanent job offer. At this point in my life, that also proved more challenging than I anticipated.

My first temporary clerical assignment was encouraging. It involved secretarial duties for a textile company that had recently relocated from Connecticut. My boss was very supportive of me, and the atmosphere was professional. This accommodating environment encouraged my best performance. The three-month assignment ended much too soon.

My second and third assignments were disasters for the hiring agency, my supervisors, and me. The computer test at the agency required only basic skills to pass, but both these assignments required advanced computer literacy. For the first time since graduation, I realized my inadequacy with computer skills. During my five plus years with Optimal Tool and Machine, I mastered a high-tech electronic typewriter while my computer skills remained dormant. I had lost most of the advanced computer skills that I learned with my degree due to lack of use. My first temporary job placement allowed me to work from a high-tech electronic typewriter, so my deficient computer skills were not a problem.

However, the responsibilities of the second and third work assignments were quite challenging, and I failed so badly I was fired. This had a devastating effect on me. I had been considered a good worker since the age of fourteen, and had only left jobs voluntarily. My involuntary dismissal from two consecutive jobs was a new and difficult experience. I decided to take refresher courses to improve my computer skills. It was beneficial, but, to this day, the computer is not my strength, and I have come to believe this is because of my brain injury.

With a record of two consecutively failed temporary assignments, I was sure the temporary agency would terminate my employment. To my amazement, I was given a fourth assignment, though it was condescending. It did not require any secretarial skills, but I accepted it since something was better than nothing.

Meanwhile, Joseph's application for medical disability was in process, and he was having second thoughts about retiring from the workforce. Long months of unemployment and mediocre temporary positions that led to dead ends started to have an effect on me. He began to fantasize about relocating to Florida where the advantages for small machine shops were more promising. One of his friends, who operated his own machine shop in Florida, had been encouraging this idea of a second machine shop.

Considering Joseph's declining health, I was not exactly thrilled by the new idea. We agreed to give it some time. He was still occupied by selling the wide accumulation of tools, machines, and equipment from both motorcycle shop and machine shop. This kept him occupied and helped us to stay financially afloat.

The end of my fourth temporary job marked the beginning of my worst period of unemployment in many years. I expanded my search and applied at several temporary agencies, but my job placements remained useless. I was bored and depressed with my situation and did not come out of it until a strange encounter with my very close friend Brother Woodward. One day, Joseph, Brother Woodward, and I were involved in a discussion, and I thought that our friend spoke to us in a very condescending way. My response was a reaction to this opinion. Though I did not swear or insult him, my tone of voice and my body language took on its own condescending attitude toward him.

I did not know I was capable of this behavior, and was convinced that I would be subject to the consequences. In a few weeks, when Brother Woodward asked for my help with his construction business, I accepted the offer. I saw it as a way to make amends. I do not know if I ever apologized to Brother Woodward in person as I should have for my gross misconduct, but I am truly sorry for it.

> I firmly believed that as soon as I learned the lesson He wanted to teach me, God would rescue me from the storm.

However, when I stepped up to my self-proclaimed punishment, I soon discovered that construction work is not an easy job. Climbing ladders, painting, and roofing were tiresome and difficult. On the worst day I had to work on the roofing task I had been assigned and wondered what I had gotten myself into.

My dirty appearance at the end of the day was not pleasant to my husband. He did not understand why I was doing this job, and neither did my family. All three of my sisters constantly called me, trying to understand my behavior.

"Rita, how do you think this will affect your mother?" one of them finally asked, when nothing else worked.

"Well, I hope you will not tell her," I replied.

For a moment, I did think about her question. I remembered how Mom did not let me skip, run, or climb trees because she was overly protective of my facial problem. Yet, concern for my mom did not influence me enough to quit construction work.

Despite the frequent criticism, I continued in this difficult job, convinced that I would be delivered in God's time. No one but God and I knew I saw this work as providential chastisement for my haughty spirit. I firmly believed that as soon as I learned the lesson He wanted to teach me, God would rescue me from the storm. Not only did He rescue me from the physical storm of construction work, He rescued me from the psychological and emotional storm that had unknowingly held me captive for twenty-six years.

The malady that imprisoned me for so long was the failure to forgive another person, whether knowingly or unknowingly. It was my denial of the passive anger I carried around for so many years that led me through much pain and suffering. Once my denial was broken, I was able to recognize myself as my own deceiver and discover the pain I had caused to myself and those around me.

My defining moment finally came during this humbling experience of my life. One cold winter night, I arrived home feeling too ashamed and despondent to talk with anyone, including Joseph. Whenever I asked for time by myself, Joseph would remind me of the time when we were getting acquainted.

"I can still hear you asking, 'Is anyone sitting here?'" he said. "And if I remember correctly, you were glad when I said 'No,' and that you could sit with me."

"That's because you looked so pitiful and alone," was always my response.

That Thursday night, not even Joseph could break through my despair. I was finally able to find the courage to return a call to Martha. During our conversation, my strong, persevering personality, which I always used to cover my true emotions did not impress my big sister. She knew how much I dreaded cold, wet winters. She must have been convinced that despite my words, I was uncomfortable with my work. Of course, Joseph did not spare anybody, especially Martha, the pitiful and disturbing details of my choice of work.

That night, Martha spoke some words that caught my attention. I did not instantaneously contemplate them, but they stuck with me.

"Rita, you've always wanted to get into social work," Martha said. "Why not now? Without a steady family income, you will qualify for financial aid. So, why not now?"

"I think you are right," I agreed. This may be a good time. I will give it some thought."

It must have been the Holy Spirit motivating my words because I was not truly interested at the moment. I was too tired to give Martha an honest, well thought out response. It was possible that I could have forgotten or ignored her advice altogether.

My return to work the following Monday put me back on the miserable roof. In the middle of that horrible, back-braking work came Martha's voice asking, "Why not now?"

"Why not now?" I asked myself. It was then that I finally realized the explanation for my stressful, rollercoaster of life experiences relating to my search for work. I feel that this moment was Divinely laid out for me. It was revealed that I had never forgiven that interviewer in St. Lucia who had denied me a secretarial position simply because of my facial features.

Throughout my struggles in the years after that painful incident, I expected God to resolve my problems immediately without taking into account the way God uses our difficulties to refine us and build our character. However, unlike Joseph, Abraham, Daniel, and Moses who all underwent trials and learned from them, I felt it took me too many years of trials to learn the simple error that, small as it was, had been the focus of most of my life.

This is my personal affirmation that although I failed God so intensely during most of my life's experiences, like Moses, I was able to turn to God. His grace is sufficient for me too. I was also blessed to realize that God's ideal vocation for me was in the field of human services.

Until this time my selfish, revenge-seeking goal of becoming an executive secretary permeated my brain. I remained imprisoned by someone else's flippant remark about my face for most of my life. My inability to forgive this offense resulted in tunnel vision that left me with zero insight into God's true will for my career.

Thinking back on this matter, I do not recall ever bringing my secretarial career to God. Yet, I assumed he sanctioned it. God allowed me many years of processing before I learned that my perception of Him had been inaccurate in this matter. Until that time, I encountered many disappointing, humiliating, debilitating, and near death experiences.

Prior to that painful interview in St. Lucia, my ideal long-term goal was a career in human services. By overlooking forgiveness, I overlooked one of the primary requirements of my faith:

"For if you forgive others for their transgressions, your heavenly Father will also forgive you. But if you do not forgive others, then your Father will not forgive your transgressions" (Matt. 6:14, 15).

"Bearing with one another, and forgiving each other, whoever has a complaint against anyone; just as the Lord forgave you, so also should you" (Col. 3:13).

"But one whom you forgive anything, I forgive also; for indeed what I have forgiven, if I have forgiven anything, I did it for your sakes in the presence of Christ, so that no advantage would be taken of us by Satan, for we are not ignorant of his schemes" (2 Cor. 2:10, 11).

In order to forgive, we must control out thoughts as Paul again points out: "We are destroying speculations and every lofty thing raised up against the knowledge of God, and we are taking every thought captive to the obedience of Christ" (2 Cor. 10:5).

I found the book *Mental and Emotional Health* by Julian Melgosa to be most helpful in understanding these passages.

On Forgiveness

God supplies forgiveness to His children, so they can improve their relationships. Both spiritual and religious counselors include forgiveness with prayer, singing, reading of God's Word, worshiping, and journaling as techniques for improving and healing oneself. Psychologists have not always recognized the importance of forgiveness, but now even secular counselors consider it to be important, and arguments for it are found in professional literature.

Forgiveness allows people to put aside and overcome issues and problems of the past while enhancing their general positive feelings, repairing lost relationships, and unloading hostility that can become a heavy psychological burden. Even in cases of spousal abandonment, reputations ruined by gossip, wrongfully dismissed employees, and those betrayed through financial scams, forgiveness can improve lives. Holding grudges and fighting back can be expensive in terms of mental health. Vengeance seldom resolves anything and even less frequently provides any benefit.

For the Believer, forgiveness makes us one step closer to following in Jesus' footsteps, as Ephesians 4:32 states, "Be kind to one another, tender-hearted, forgiving each other, just as God in Christ also has forgiven you."

As a Person Thinks

Consider the following passage that was written by Ellen G. White titled "Right-Thinking." It appeared in the August 23, 1905, edition of *The Signs of the Times*.

More precious than the golden wedge of Ophir is the power of right thought. We need to place a high value upon the right control of our thoughts; for such control prepares us to labor for the Master. It is necessary for our peace and happiness in this life that our thoughts center in Christ. As a man thinketh, so is he.

The merciful shall find mercy, and the pure in heart shall see God. Every impure thought defiles the soul, impairs the moral sense, and tends to obliterate the impressions of the Holy Spirit. It dims the spiritual vision, so that men cannot behold God....

Evil thoughts destroy the soul. The converting power of God changes the heart, refining and purifying the thoughts. Unless a determined effort is made to keep the thoughts centered on Christ, grace cannot reveal itself in the life. The mind must engage in the spiritual warfare. Every thought must be brought into captivity to the obedience of Christ. All the habits must be brought under God's control.

We need a constant sense of the ennobling power of pure thoughts and the damaging influence of evil thoughts. Let us place our thoughts on holy things. Let them be pure and true, for the only security for any soul is right thinking. We are to use every means that God has placed within our reach for the government and cultivation of our thoughts. We are to bring our minds into harmony with Christ's mind. His truth will sanctify us, body, soul, and spirit and we shall be enabled to rise above temptation.

In brief, our thoughts will determine our behavior; deeds that are both good and bad originate in the heart rather than from external forces.

Unwholesome Thinking

When our thoughts become distressing, people can tell. There is an old Spanish proverb that says, "*La cara es el espejo del alma*" (The face is the mirror of the soul).

When one has distressful thoughts for long periods of time, it can lead to unstable behaviors. It is important for people to avoid the wrong kind of thinking just as much as it is important to avoid certain behaviors and sins. Each of these things can affect the other and create a downward spiral that is difficult to recover from. It is important to note that the Christian approach to avoiding evil needs to be both internal and external.

> ... our thoughts will determine our behavior; deeds that are both good and bad originate in the heart rather than from external forces.

Wholesome Thinking

According to the apostle Paul, we need to dwell on wholesome thoughts rather than evil ones. Philippians 4:8 states: "Finally, brethren, whatever is true, whatever is honorable, whatever is right, whatever is pure, whatever is lovely, whatever is of good repute, if there is any excellence and if anything worthy of praise, dwell on these things."

The emphasis is placed upon some sort of cognitive task—thinking, understanding, reasoning, comparing and contrasting, memorizing, observing cause-effect relationships, and applying principles to practice. Paul was appealing to all his readers to stick to Scriptures as the sure way of keeping a safe mental outlook.

The lyrics of "Forgiveness" by Christian artist Matthew West explain the difference in the effects of experiencing and extending forgiveness. It is a powerful song that resonated with my feelings.

Though we usually see forgiveness as losing, the reality is that those who forgive are winning. Forgiveness is about losing oneself in order to gain a Christlike character, which is the sweetest, most triumphant victory one can experience. The result of actively seeking a Christlike character is internal, external, and spiritual wellness. These in turn lead to self-growth and maturity.

This enlightened perspective was not yet revealed to me on that formidable, cold winter day, when my hands were too numb to feel the thud of a hammer as it pounded away at near frozen nails. It simply occurred to me how far I had strayed from my original life goals because I was consumed by and controlled by a human being, who had refused me a job because of my disfigured face.

That day when I decided, "I will prove you wrong—I will be the best, most effective secretary who ever lived," I left the real me behind. In the years that followed, I became so consumed by my drive, determination, and struggles against the adversities I faced, both real and imagined, that I completely lost sight of my original passion.

Although my conviction about my inability to forgive my offender did not come until almost decades later, I was not spared the effects of my censure. Forgiveness cannot only add to and improve your process of healing from wrongs that were done to you but it can also help you release anger in a productive way.

Looking back, it is easy to see how I could have handled the interview in a healthier way. The way I reacted was far from God's ideal of forgiveness. It is perfectly acceptable to experience pain and anger over something, as long as we go on to deal with those emotions. Pain and anger tell us something is wrong. Once we know something is wrong, we have the choice of how to deal with it.

My response to that wrong deed, in the case of the interviewer, should have been genuine forgiveness. Instead, I shuffled from my offender's presence, determined to prove him wrong. This attitude resulted in decades of disappointment and robbed me of an opportunity to experience the Divine healing that comes from the process of forgiveness. I firmly believe that nothing passes God unnoticed and nothing happens to God's children by coincidence, good or bad. If there had been a less painful way to connect me with God's ideal of forgiveness, I believe that God would have used it. After all, His love for fallen humans surpasses the love provided by an earthly father.

In time, I learned to appreciate this lesson of forgiveness instead of resorting to vengeance. Taking any kind of vengeance is a form of putting other gods before the Lord. This may sound extreme until it is understood in the context of Scripture. In fact, the Bible is punctuated with several texts indicating vengeance is God's responsibility. It does not matter if our vengeance is subtle or passive or outright.

It may be something as simple as refusing to help our offender because we feel that he or she is getting what he or she deserves. No matter what, we are taking God's role upon ourselves.

Who are we to act for God? No one, who fears Him would dare to think of playing God. Yet, so many Christians find it difficult to forgive others because they do not realize that their failure to forgive is in itself a form of vengeance and therefore disobedience to God. Holding grudges only results in a life without hope and meaning, a life in direct contrast to God's ideal of wellness.

Instead of playing God, I need to pray for the opportunity to partner with God to rescue the perishing. It is a very serious matter, but self is forever seeking to trivialize or confuse my understanding of it. For instance, I have learned that forgiveness always involves wisdom and discernment, not enabling. There were times when, in my ignorance and confusion, I enabled with the intention of forgiving. The result was chaos for me and everyone else involved.

I offer the following scenario to show a contrast between enabling and forgiveness:

Dan, an only son, is second to his father's heart after God. Because of this, Dan is dearly loved but was not spared the discipline he needed. He was taught right from wrong on an age appropriate level. Even through his difficult teen years, Dan remained true to his Christian virtues. However, at age twenty-one, Dan began keeping company with unbelievers, and his behavior changed drastically for the worse.

One night, when Dan broke his curfew again, his father was awakened by a late telephone call from a police officer that informed him of the most unwelcome news. Dan had been arrested because he was with his law-breaking peers. The father's initial thought was, *Leave him there—he knew better.*

After praying and pondering, the father was motivated to bail Dan out and even paid his fines. He thought, *Everyone is capable of making a mistake and learning from the outcome. I will allow him to work and pay me back so he does not take this for granted.*

Dan returned to the pretense of "abiding by the rules." Nevertheless, he soon returned to his pattern of breaking the rules and following self-destructive pursuits. Another night, the telephone rang hours after Dan's curfew, and the father suspected bad news on the other end. Dan had been arrested again.

This time the father thought, *I will leave him to experience the bitter consequences of his actions. He will spend restless, sleepless nights on the cement bunks of his cell. It breaks my heart, but to go to his rescue would enable him to continue his unacceptable behavior unchecked. By not paying his bail, I am supporting him. I am allowing him an opportunity to realize his need to change his lifestyle. To continuously rescue him is to enable him to continue his self-destructive behavior. By allowing him to face the consequences of his behavior, I am supporting him.*

We can understand why the enemy works overtime to keep us in ignorance or in confusion when we realize that forgiveness is a providential attribute for the wellness of body, mind, and spirit for both grantors and recipients. Like all other Christlike virtues, we must look to Christ and be led by his Word and His Holy Spirit in our willingness to forgive. Otherwise, we may find ourselves grossly enabling and doing more harm than good in the situation. It is frequently easier to enable loved ones and seek vengeance upon those who are not close to us than it is to forgive either of the two with discernment and wisdom.

Chapter 19

Many More Rivers to Cross

Although my defining moment served as my great spiritual awakening, which brought many opportunities my way, life was still full of obstacles. In fact, I have faced even more turbulent challenges since then. However, the result is that I am more dependent on a Savior who knows how to pilot me safely through the angry waves, as John E. Gould wrote, when he composed the song "Jesus, Savior, Pilot Me." Additionally, the lingering consequences of my gross error further validate the certainty of God's fatherly attributes. Hebrews 12:5–10 states:

> And you have forgotten the exhortation which is addressed to you as sons, "My son, do not regard lightly the discipline of the Lord, nor faint when you are reproved by Him; for those whom the Lord loves He disciplines, and He scourges every son whom He receives." It is for discipline that you endure; God deals with you as with sons; for what son is there whom His father does not discipline? But if you are without discipline, of which all have become partakers, then you are illegitimate children and not sons. Furthermore, we had earthly fathers to discipline us, and we respected them; shall we not much rather be subject to the Father of spirits, and live? For they disciplined us for a short time as seemed best to them, but He disciplines us for our good, so that we may share His holiness.

This was my frame of mind in 1995 when I entered Anderson College (now Anderson University) to pursue a bachelor's degree in psychology within two to three years. I thought I would transfer my credits from Tri-County Technical College. Unfortunately, in my ignorance of how the system worked, none of my credits were transferrable to an accredited four-year college. So, I braced myself for more than four years of study.

Toward the ending of my first college semester, my psychology professor stated that people who have sustained a brain injury could not perform college

"For those whom the Lord loves He disciplines, and He scourges every son whom He receives."

work. That was an immediate red flag for me. Still leaning on the Lord, but cognizant of my ability to err, I thought, *Lord, what am I doing here?*

After much praying, I thought I needed to change my major to something less challenging for my traumatized brain. It later occurred to me that the enemy also works to discourage us. I consulted with an advisor, but I did not inform her of my brain injury and any issues that might cause. Instead, I told her that I needed to graduate as soon as possible in order to pursue stable employment. She informed me of a social service program that required only limited credits in psychology. However, this new course of study required several credits in the arts, so I considered three classes with highest credit options. One of these classes was "The Theatre."

I did not have an interest in the theatre, but I did want to take a course with more credits to help me get through more quickly. To my surprise, I understood the objective of this theater course and it was evident by my class work. The professor often commended my progress. In a private meeting at the end of the semester the professor asked, "Are you sure you do not want to go further into the theatre? You are so good at it."

For a moment, the childhood fantasies of Hollywood rushed through my mind, and I could hear self's acoustic assurance, *This is your opportunity.* Thankfully, I remembered where my vain, self-centered pursuits had taken me. Without hesitating I smiled and said, "Thank you so much for your vote of confidence, but I have an urgent need for employment. Maybe, that will come someday."

I continued this course of study at Anderson College for two years. During these two years, I was challenged with another offer from two English professors. Coincidentally, one of these professors worked with Tri-County Technical College, and was my English professor there as well. He still remembered my writing aptitude and advised me to consider a career in writing. The other Anderson College English professor encouraged me to do the same. At the end of all my graded papers, the second professor wrote a note commending my writing skills and urging me to contemplate a writing career. These commendations were affirming because I had been resisting my providential conviction to write my life story. However, a full-fledged career in writing was not part of my short-term, or even my distant, future plan.

Things were uneventful for several years, but the following experience is what convinced me that God had not approved of my change in majors. It is a micro example of the great controversy between God and the devil that started from the beginning. It also shows how the intensity of this controversy can, at times, result in our temporary inability to see God's hand upon our lives.

I was about to register for one of my last two semesters when it occurred to me that I was at a dead end road. I had completed all my required credits. I did not want to pursue a theatre or writing career, so I had a problem deciding on how to use up my elective credits. This should not have been a big deal, but it was to me. I turned to prayer and was convinced to pursue a four-year degree. Anderson College had an extremely high tuition, so I considered Clemson University. To my initial dismay, my nearly completed curriculum at Anderson College was not offered at Clemson University. I consulted with an advisor and learned that with a few more classes in psychology, I could consider a major in sociology, which would give me a good foundation for employment in human services. I could follow my degree with postgraduate studies in social work if I wanted.

At this point in my college career, I welcomed this option without a thought to whether or not my brain injury would be a barrier to psychological studies. I now attribute my willingness to God's timing. While the devil continued to work against me, God was always stronger.

The various challenges I encountered during my three years at Clemson University were enough to make me lose any desire for a postgraduate degree. With a course load of at least twelve credit hours per semester and at least two hours of respite service four days of the week, my home responsibilities and inadequacies relating to my memory problems plagued me. Many times I felt my prayers went unheard. Often, when at my worst, it was a professor's act of kindness or some unexpected occurrence that served to remind me God is always present.

Consider my struggles in Western Heritage. On the first day of class, the professor announced she was not the type of professor to cut anyone slack. All the papers were required to be turned in on or before due dates, and tests and finals required a lot of memorization of important dates. I was apprehensive then, and throughout the semester, because of my inability to effectively retain and retrieve certain information.

I spent most of my study time on the material for this class. However by the final exam, my grade was a low C. I was overwhelmed. I would need a high B on the final to pass, and I could not imagine doing that.

The stress negatively impacted my progress in my other three classes, where I managed to maintain one A and a strong B. My grade in Spanish was similar to my Western Heritage class. The only difference was that my Spanish professor was more lenient.

The day of the Western Heritage final, I was sleep deprived and nervous. The announcement of "time's up" came much too soon. I had struggled only halfway through the exam and was overwhelmingly concerned that most of my answers were incorrect. When the second-to-last student handed in her exam and left me alone in my state of helplessness, I decided it was time to have a talk with my professor. It was difficult to hold back the tears as I briefly informed her of my accident, and the problems I experienced with both long- and short-term memory. Surprisingly, this tyrant professor responded with enthusiasm. She took the time to encourage me and then ended by saying, "Take as much time as you need." In addition, she shared with me that Dr. Harley also had an accident that resulted in memory problems.

At the beginning of the semester, I noticed a uniquely, quiet, middle-aged female that everyone addressed by the title of "doctor." I wondered why this woman was here with undergraduates. About midway through the class, Dr. Harley stopped attending. In contrast to my memory loss, Dr. Harley lost enough memory to affect her inability to perform at a doctoral level, so she was attempting to repeat her undergraduate studies. Her memory problems were so severe that she had to drop out of college. I realized I had no reason to suffer self-pity, and I should be counting my blessings. In the next forty minutes I completed the last half of the exam, reviewed it, corrected the first half, and thankfully handed it over. My gracious professor responded warmly. I received a high C in the class, but it felt like an A to me.

My high C in Spanish 101 made me reconsider my desire for a bachelor of arts degree instead of a bachelor of science degree. The latter did not require the four semesters of foreign language that the former did. I realistically assessed my time and knew I did not have what was required to obtain any level of fluency in foreign language. I quickly changed to a bachelor of science.

Encouraging and challenging moments in my academic career continued to occur side-by-side. I struggled in my studies and frequently contemplated giving up. However, I persisted because I felt a Power much bigger than me that would not allow me to surrender. Unlike the first two years, I was too preoccupied with my studies to keep track of time. On May 12, 2000, I graduated with a bachelor's degree in sociology, a minor in psychology, and a certificate in substance abuse and education. I began this certification to support my brother, who was chemically dependent, but by the end, I was convinced that it was for my much needed healing.

Years before when I first discovered my brother's addiction to alcohol, it was difficult to understand why everyone thought my emotional response was an overreaction. My Mom kept assuring me there was no need to cry.

"Jacob is not dead," she said. "He just had too much to drink."

Of course, no one knew that my response stemmed from emotions of pain, disgust, fear, and a great deal of anger from my first experience of alcoholism in my uncle. I was angry with Jacob for allowing this into the shelter of our family.

If there is any truth to the saying, "Time is a great healer," it did not apply to my brother's situation. Time was not on his side. He went from weekend drunkenness to weekday intoxication. My feelings of anger and frustration were intensified with genuine concern for him. Despite my personal aversion to alcohol, I made Jacob my primary concern. Many nights I lay awake quietly drenching my pillow with tears while listening for my brother's arrival. He frequently stayed out all night.

As if Jacob's drunkenness were not complicated enough, he began to act oddly even when he was not drunk. For example, he would show up at my job wearing bizarre clothing. I did not have the nerve to ignore him, but being around him was humiliating. I often wondered what my friends thought of him, but most importantly, what they thought about me for having a brother like him. I was too naïve to realize my brother was using other mood-altering drugs.

My migration to the United States was the first time I had a break from my relationship with my chemically dependent brother. The geographical distance and the fact that he did not write made it impossible to maintain contact with him. I only knew what came through in the letters of my other relatives.

Shortly after my departure from St. Lucia, Jacob moved to St. Thomas in the Virgin Islands. We heard that he had stopped drinking. However, after his marriage failed, he drifted back to his alcoholic lifestyle which resulted in major trouble with the law.

Empowered by faith and God's strength, Martha was able to make a trip to St. Thomas. There, she found Jacob living in dire poverty and faced with several alcohol-related charges including driving under the influence and driving with a suspended license. Jacob's frailty and near-death appearance, combined with his legal problems, seemed beyond human intervention. However, God had other plans.

Martha was able to convince the judge that our brother could rectify his life, because he came from a good family that would support him. She pleaded for the charges to be dropped. In exchange, she promised to take Jacob to the United States and assist him with the support needed for his recovery. The judge considered my sister's request, and our prayers were answered. The charges were dropped contingent on his willingness to leave with Martha. The judge made it clear that if he returned to St. Thomas, it would result in his immediate arrest and detention.

My husband and I were childless, but Martha was raising two children. It was more convenient for Jacob to reside with us, so we took him into our home. After months of rehabilitation, Jacob's condition improved remarkably. I was feeling comfortable about his recovery when family arranged for Jacob to visit them in Canada. I still recall the glitter in his eyes and his enthusiasm as he boarded his flight. He was, again, the brother I knew before the onset of his alcoholism. *Thank God*, I thought. *We are winning this fight.*

Unfortunately, at the end of Jacob's stay in Canada, he told me he had decided to move to Brooklyn. He intended to live with one of our alcoholic cousins. I tried to persuade him to reconsider his decision, but his mind was set. He thought he had a better chance to live a successful life in Brooklyn. He did not recognize the daily temptation he would be exposed to by living with another alcoholic. I hoped he would keep his promise of abstinence, but I feared for him.

Shortly after Jacob's arrival in Brooklyn, he was involved in an alcohol- and drug-related bust that led to his arrest and short-term imprisonment. I refused to feel guilty for not running to my brother's rescue. I may have forgiven him for his errors, but I knew it was time to step back and let him experience the consequences of his behavior.

My response led me to acknowledge that genuine concern for others does not lead to selfish endeavors. Pitying and mothering him did nothing to truly help him; it only made me feel better because I was playing an active part in keeping him away from alcohol. I had to find other alternatives for dealing with my painful experiences.

My training in abnormal psychology and substance abuse helped to broaden my perspective about my brother's alcoholism, and also about how alcohol-impacted my past. Based upon the nature of his illness, I realize Jacob had the choice to step out of that lifestyle and get help or to remain in his condition and continue to suffer the consequences. I have not given up hope that Jacob will eventually make the right choice, but I have prepared myself to deal with the worst possible outcome of his condition.

Looking back on my motivation for considering my substance abuse certification, I see God's leading in two ways. My initial motivation was to further support my brother's recovery. It turned out this program aided my continued healing and began my training as a certified addictions counselor. Sadly, Jacob has yet to return from Brooklyn, and I am uncertain whether he is dead or alive.

Chapter 20

This Grave Injustice

May of 2000 marked almost twenty-four years since my last departure from St. Lucia. I felt detached from my roots. In addition, the death of loved ones convinced me that time passes very quickly. I also felt it was time to acquaint Joseph with the difference between a tropical and a southern climate.

We scheduled our St. Lucian vacation for June, approximately one month after my graduation from Clemson University. Other than occasionally thinking about the fact that my father would not be there, planning the trip was exciting. We looked forward to a well-deserved break from our lives and had a non-verbalized understanding to return with increased motivation. We wanted to reconstruct the fragments of our lives for God's honor and glory. This remained our resonating conviction throughout the three weeks spent in St. Lucia.

I noticed positive differences in Joseph's overall demeanor while there particularly in his relationship with me. He appeared to be enjoying every moment of life. In addition to his special welcome by my family, friends, and relatives, every aspect of my West Indian culture captivated him except for what he called the crazy drivers. He exclaimed in awe about the lofty hills, the vast, sky-blue ocean forever peaking with gentle waves, and, especially, the dense array of vegetation and fruits. The unending sights of tall trees laden with coconuts, mangoes, and other fruits made him wonder how anyone could go hungry with all the food in St. Lucia.

"Well," I replied practically, "there are people like me whose taste buds like foreign foods such as rice and pasta." My effort to correct his perception fell on deaf ears. We walked in the golden rays of sunset and welcomed the early mornings' warm sunlight on Gros Islet's sandy beach.

Our departure time came much too soon especially for Joseph, who wished to take St. Lucia's frequent drizzles of rain and tropical sunlight with him. However, Joseph was not impressed with the drivers on the island, despite the fact that he arrived safely to every destination. He wanted to bestow on St. Lucian drivers his idea of safe, defensive driving skills.

Although saddened by good-byes, our return flight was an equally enjoyable experience. We had so much to talk and laugh about from our trip. At this point, we agreed to visit our St. Lucian family and friends every two or three years. Joseph also resolved to pursue his interest in organic gardening and resume his invention of a collapsible plant hanger upon our return. I sighed in relief, because I would return to search for a job and not to studying for an exam or complete a research paper. Joseph did not delay his gardening project. Shortly following our return, the sound of his dirt-hungry garden tractor appealed to him once more.

I had worked part-time during college for a government agency, and they proceeded to hire me for a full-time position. Although my full-time work performance and pay were below what my education demanded, I accepted the position, because I would be the first person considered when a director position came open in my department.

I had seen many trials in my life up to this point and frequently asked the question, "Why, Lord?" When suffering the storms of life, this is a common question for people. Even Job could not fathom the depths or reasons for what happened to him. God is omniscient and has many more reasons for doing things than our human minds could begin to understand. I believe that in general, the answer to this question comes down to the need to develop a trusting faith with a spirit of total surrender. This is a day-by-day process for me.

Jeremiah 2:13 says, "For My people have committed two evils: They have forsaken Me, the fountain of living waters, to hew for themselves cisterns, broken cisterns that can hold no water."

I am convinced that to live my life in pursuit of anything outside of God's will is the same as if I made broken cisterns for myself. My plans may have been intended to form something useful, but in the end it was useless because I did not listen to the plan of the One who knows how best to care for me. God is a good Father, letting me know when I have strayed. His grace is sufficient for those times to bring me back into the fold.

Even now, after all the many lessons I have learned, after all the pain of pursuing my goals over God's will, and after learning the importance of forgiveness, I still struggle.

In May of 2001, a year after my graduation, I submitted my résumé to my current employer. When I got the job, I was thrilled. It seemed my life had finally steered through the storm to the calm sea beyond. Despite the challenges of traveling through distant, remote areas and working with resistant clients, I thoroughly enjoyed my new job of service to the substance abuse population.

August 1, 2001, became a day of special importance that made me realize I need to take the good with the bad. First I had a remarkable day at work. One of my most resistant clients had broken through her denial. With sobs and verbalized regrets for the pain she had caused others from her addictive lifestyle, she voiced her need for rehabilitation and a drug-free lifestyle to her benefit and also her children's. With my assistance, she was able to develop a treatment plan, accented with resources to support her recovery. Elated by the result of this last home visit, I forgot to keep up with the time. In the evening's dusk, I hurried to get home while thinking about my long but meaningful day's work. I truly enjoyed it when parents made the choice to pursue an independent life and create a safe, drug-free home for their children. I was also happy to be making such a positive contribution in America, the country I perceived had contributed new meaning and purpose to my life.

Upon my arrival home, I thought it was odd that both vehicles were present but Joseph was absent. I figured that perhaps he had gone with our neighbor, Solomon, who was a carpenter with a business next door. As hours passed with no call to alert me that Joseph was okay, I began to feel queasy. I wondered what could have happened to him, and I began to run through a list of all the bad things that could have occurred.

When the phone finally rang, I snatched it up quickly. My gut feeling was one of anticipation and dread.

"Are you Mrs.—?"

"Yes, this is Mrs. Macon." I replied anxiously before the caller could complete his question.

"This is Sergeant—, and I am calling to inform you your husband Joseph Macon is here at the— Police Department. He wants you to pick him up."

I abruptly hung up the phone wondering what it could mean. I headed to the Honea Path Police Station. Then I realized that in my distress, I had failed to listen and to let the sergeant finish telling me where my husband was. My assumption about Joseph's location was wrong, and I did not even hear the sergeant's name.

In order to find my husband, I had to return home and call all the surrounding police departments. I finally located him at the Williamston Police Department. With another surge of mixed emotions, I arrived at the Williamston destination much too soon. I do not recall paying any attention to the traffic signs on my way there. The Lord must have guided and protected me that night.

As I approached the officer at the front booth, I said, "I am here to pick up my husband, Joseph Macon."

"I don't think we have anyone here by this name," the officer replied casually, "but let me check."

After one phone call, he nonchalantly informed me my husband was on his way down the stairs. Eager to see Joseph, I went to stand at the base of the stairway. I wished someone had prepared me for the unexpected condition of my husband. When he appeared, he was disheveled, moving slowly, and he fell down the last two steps.

"Joseph, didn't you see the steps?" I asked. I was already helping him struggle to his feet, but I was upset that I had not thought to give him a hand sooner.

"I can't see. They sprayed mace into my eyes. I can't see; my eyes itch and they hurt like crazy. They sprayed it on my chest too. I can't stand the burning."

"Oh, no!" I replied. I didn't know what else to say. I felt totally helpless as I helped my physically weak, sobbing, and untidy husband walk toward the car. The distinct smell of old urine filled the air. During the burdensome drive home late that night, and for many days and nights afterward, we discussed what had gone wrong on that day.

According to Joseph, around lunchtime, he needed to purchase some bolts to shorten the prototype of his invention, so he hopped on his motorcycle and headed into Williamston. He planned to stop at the seed store and the hardware store. A friend of ours had told him there was a speed trap, so he was constantly checking his speed that day. When the Honda Accord and Toyota pickup in front of him pulled over to the side of the road, Joseph looked in his mirror and saw the blue light of a police car.

Officer Beddingfield claimed Joseph was going 52 mph (according to Joseph, he was compliant with the speed limit of 35 mph. According to the trial summary, Joseph was clocked at 57 mph) in a

35 mph zone. Responding to the officer's accusation of Joseph's 52 mph speed, Joseph stated, "Officer, I know I wasn't speeding, because I had been warned, just recently, about a speed trap in Williamston, so I would not be that stupid to not watch my speed in Williamston."

Officer Beddingfield took Joseph's license and started back toward his car, but then he turned and told Joseph that he did not have a motorcycle license. Joseph had been driving his motorcycle for forty years, and he overlooked a DMV error resulting in his Class C instead of a Class DM license during his last license renewal.

When the police officer told him he was going to give him two tickets, Joseph replied that he would just have to resolve the issue in court. Like most police officers, Officer Beddingfield took a long time to write the ticket. It was during this time that Officer Brooks arrived on the scene according to his testimony. However, the mayor, Phillip E. Clardy stated that both the police officers were following Joseph. Joseph has a urological problem and suddenly had the urge to use the restroom. He told Officer Brooks, who was standing through the long wait with Joseph, that he was going to McDonalds to use the restroom. Officer Brooks did not object, so Joseph proceeded to cross the street toward McDonalds. When Joseph began to cross the street, the officers chased after him and told him he was under arrest.

"Under arrest?" Joseph asked. "What have I done to be under arrest? You said I was speeding, and I know I wasn't speeding—You said I don't have a motorcycle license—but you don't arrest anybody for speeding or not having a motorcycle license."

"Put you hands behind your back—you're under arrest for not having a motorcycle license."

"Officer," Joseph said, "I would never do anything to resist an arrest, but I have trouble with both of my shoulders, and I can't put my hands behind my back, so you will have to handcuff me from the front."

Joseph positioned his arms in front of him. Somewhere during this time, one of the officers sprayed him with mace and a city worker who had been driving along the road decided to pull over and get in the fray on the side of the police. Despite the fact that Joseph had several back and shoulder issues throughout his life, the three of them finally managed to get Joseph's arms behind him and handcuffed.

They took him to the police station and handcuffed him to the wall. By this time, my fifty-nine-year-old husband was in extreme pain from the struggle to handcuff him and the mace, and had wet on himself. When they put him in a cell, he began to feel sick. He begged the elderly officer near him for help and an EMT was brought in to check on him. At the time, his blood pressure was 198/98. They had not allowed him to call anyone but finally took his wallet and got my phone number.

This was the most humiliating, heart-wrenching experience of my life. In fact, this experience has had continuous negative, devastating impacts on Joseph's responsibilities, our marriage, and our social and spiritual life. After this experience Joseph went through not only physical but emotional pain. His shoulders, neck, and lower back region were constantly in pain that caused him trouble sleeping. This caused me sleeplessness as well. Frequently, Joseph ended up in his recliner, in the living room, so I could get at least a four-hour doze before heading into work.

Next were the MRIs that showed he would need even more surgeries on his shoulders, neck, and back. However, he could only have one surgery at a time. Since the pain in all three areas was severe, it was a difficult choice, but the neurologist explained that the shooting pain he felt in his hands originated in his neck.

Thinking he could resolve two areas of pain at once, Joseph opted for the neck surgery. Unfortunately, this created severe pain during the period of healing since he had to have three of his cervical vertebra fused with titanium. Although he took painkillers to help, it did nothing to eliminate the discomfort. Years of recovery are the only thing that has reduced some of the pain. He never returned to the doctor for the other recommended surgeries because of all the pain he suffered from this one. Joseph now lives with chronic upper and lower lumbar, cervical, and shoulder pain.

> Having to go through my own round of surgeries and emotional pain was nothing compared to the struggle of watching my husband suffer every day.

Having to go through my own round of surgeries and emotional pain was nothing compared to the struggle of watching my husband suffer every day. Having heard stories of the way people are treated by police based on the color of their skin leaves me wondering if my husband was singled out. Without my previous conviction of the positive impacts of forgiveness aforementioned, it would be harder to forgive when I only have to look at my husband's pain to see the results of this event that occurred over a decade ago.

Perhaps if the courts, set up by the Constitution had prevailed in seeing that justice was served, I would feel more at ease and open to forgiving. Unlike the man who claimed I would never be a secretary, these men have faces and represent positions of authority that I may have to deal with again in my life.

I wish I could say this incident did not impact my faith negatively, but it did. However, I no longer ask, "Why, Lord?" Instead, I continuously turn to God's Word for comfort. My primary consolation comes from Romans 8:28, "And we know that God causes all things to work together for good to those who love God, to those who are called according to His purpose."

During my past struggles and trials, I have grown in my personal knowledge of God and the reality of his love. Although I have yet to understand the reason for this grave act of injustice, I can still trust in God. Most importantly, I now find it difficult not to trust the God I love. My trust in Him annuls my questions.

In order to avoid my inclination to misjudge the police officers, the Lord allowed me an encounter with an officer whose intervention was nothing less than life saving. Shortly before signing the contract for publication of this manuscript, my sister and I had an early morning telephone discussion regarding her son's bipolar issues and my husband's traumatic brain injury ramifications. Although we ended the discussion with prayer, I failed to leave my concerns at Calvary.

I had an 8:00 a.m. appointment the same day with a very resistant client. To best prepare for the day's challenge, I left home an hour and a half earlier than usual so I could get to work an hour early. I was not in a hurry and was surprised when I was pulled over for driving ten miles over the speed limit. I also failed to stop at the stop sign. It did not take long for me to realize that I must have been too preoccupied with family life issues to focus on my driving. I apologized to the officer and briefly informed her of my failure to leave my family's problems at the cross. She advised me to show up in court and see what happens.

The following points are important lessons I learned from this embarrassing incident: I am a more conscientious and safe driver when I allow my faith in God to work out my family problems. I can validate my belief that all police officers are not inhumane or prejudiced. Standing before the judge and praying about my fate, I heard the unfamiliar response of "No processing, your honor," from my police officer. While still pondering the meaning of her statement, the judge smiled and stated, "Your officer requested 'No processing.' You are free to go Ms. Macon."

Acknowledgements

I am thankful for all the individuals who give my life meaning in the midst of life's storms. I am aware that each person's contribution is an indication of God's love and care. I wish to extend appreciation to the many individuals, past and present, whose choices continue to inspire my willingness to live and contribute in this life.

First and foremost, I wish to show my deepest appreciation to Mr. Bartholomew Gaspard (my school master) and his wife. It is important that I extend appreciation to his wife, because I remember my feelings of jealousy when my Sir got married. She was beautiful, and I thought she would not tolerate an ugly-face girl in her home. Surprisingly, I was wrong. Even after the birth of their first child, Grace, I continued to experience a sense of belonging with the Gaspard family. I doubt that Mr. Gaspard knew he was infusing me with the hope that I so desperately needed when, at age ten, he informed me of the possibility of advanced medical treatment in the United States. In addition to this message of hope, I attribute my core values of determination, steadfastness, perseverance and balance to lessons learned from Sir during my childhood.

Secondly, I want to extend much appreciation to members of my biological family who continue to love me unconditionally. They have learned how important it is to love me without infringing on my independence. My sincere appreciation goes to Martha, our eldest sibling, for her dedication and strong example of faith, fortitude, and character.

To my sister Jessica, you picked up where Martha left off.

I especially thank God for my husband Joseph. Joseph, my dear, you keep me on my knees, and that is always a good place for me.

I still hold my memories of Mount Sinai Hospital staff of 1973 very dear. I particularly remember the chief of radiologist, my doctor, and his family. I will also always appreciate the friends and prayer warriors from Faith Church, my first church home in America. The late Pastor Jerry Lee, who baptized me; Pastor Keith Dennis, my father-figure; the board of elders, particularly the late Elder Earle, my great admirer and inspirer; the Campbell family; the Prayer Group, and many more of Faith Church's families who adopted me into their families and were very instrumental in my rich and continued spiritual growth.

I cannot forget the faithful lawyer who transported me to the immigration office at the end of every six months and assisted me with an extended visa at no cost to me. I must acknowledge, too, the

Heinz family, whose daughter Joyce introduced me to this God-fearing lawyer. I also appreciate my sister's employers whose generosity influenced my easy admission and care by Mount Sinai Hospital. All these unmerited favors indicated God's presence with me and fostered my resolve to live.

I have, in my memory bank, strong affirmations by Pastor Dunte Tobias, who once said to me, "Sister Macon, everything you do, you do so well." (I doubt if he remembers saying this but it deeply impacted me.) Imagine how much these words meant to me, coming from a childhood where my abilities were belittled and deemed unworthy. My affiliation with Pastor Drake Barber and his family, particularly his wife Brenda, remains a rich blessing.

I would also like to acknowledge Elder Sherrod and his wife, Pat. In fact, God used Elder Sherrod, decades ago, to water that seed of faith about writing my autobiography. At the end of a Sabbath School lesson study during a married couple's retreat at Cohutta Springs, I was surprised when Elder Sherrod called me to the side and commented about my conduct of the lesson study. In addition to his words of admiration and commendation, he asked me the question, "Sister Macon, have you ever thought about writing a book about your life?" Here, again, God was partnering with a human being to bless and inspire me. I answered Pastor Sherrod's question in the affirmative because I already knew God required this of me. Yet, I remained reluctant.

I am thankful, too, for the ministry of Pastor Nixon, Jr., and his wife, April. Pastor Nixon, your sermons were no less impacting to me than your words of affirmation. Most importantly, you provided a confidential listening ear and Christlike responses to my problems. I am also thankful for Pastor Ronnie Williams and his dear wife, Monica. Pastor Williams, your down-to-earth attitude and love for people further enriched my life. Sister Williams, your gentle, yet determined spirit, and your deep-belly laugh made the burdens lighter. Thanks, too, for my much-undeserved presents, but beyond all of this, for letting me see Jesus in you.

My list of inspirational pastors and their wives now includes Pastor Carl Nesmith and his loving wife. Their rewarding works of faith further motivate and inspire me to continue walking by faith and not by sight.

On the horizontal level of church ministry, I have been favored with the support of church families like the late Brother Claude Jones and his living wife, Nettie. I still have among my prized possessions their inspirational cards with messages of hope for Joseph and me. How could they have known which cards to pick and mail at times most appropriate unless they were partnering with God?

I want to extend my appreciation to my truest friends, Marian Gray and her family. Now that I am nearing the ending of this manuscript, I am thankful for Marian's constant reminder that she is anxiously waiting to read my book. (Although I must confess, sometimes, I wished she would let me forget.)

To our former Married Couples' Club, the wonderful memories together and your support during my near-death accident will never be forgotten. Dr. Albert Bartholomew, thoughts about your dedication in delivering the nutritional, delightful meals, so tediously prepared by your wife (who is now deceased), not to mention your traveling time and monetary cost for the approximate seventy-mile round trip, are still delightfully stunning.

I would like to thank the many other church families and friends who have blessed my life. Elder and Sister Dawkins, your lives are truly an inspiration to me. Sister Solomon, and Sister Harrison, Sisters Noel, Marie, Nellie, and Cindy, we go back such a long way, and our God has kept us afloat through so many of life's storms. Many thanks to April, too, for my constant inspiring e-mail verses.

Brother Woodward, thanks again for my lesson on the roof. "Lil, we are a long ways from Tri-County."

Elder and Sister Harold Griffin and family, thanks for sharing your Sabbath dinners with us—we especially enjoyed the Sabbath fellowship.

To Brother and Sister Leon Bonaparte, and to Brother Gillian Bonaparte and his wife, Barbara, Elder and Sister Limehouse, Brother Curtis Wayne and his wife, Tammie. You, too, have inspired me to keep trusting God.

To my late-on-the-scene friends, Jimmy Mims and Marjorie Foster, your prayers and support have proven that friends in need are friends indeed.

To members of Anderson First and Zion Temple, Spartanburg and Toccoa Church, and members of North 81 Church, our affiliation has drawn me closer to God.

I would also like to show my appreciation for the South Atlantic Conference representatives, including the humble Walker family. Our various times of work and fellowship, enjoying simple, delicious meals, left us with the impression that each fellowship is a miniature experience of the ultimate celebration at the second coming. Our ability to weather the storms of life is the direct result of your prayers and godly influence.

To my current telephone prayer conference group, thanks for your fervent love and inspiration. Together we will continue to weather the storms of life, inspired always by the ultimate hope of a glorious outcome awaiting us at the second coming.

Without exception, the positive influence outside of my church family has been very impacting. I have great admiration for my College Professors from Tri-County, Anderson College (now Anderson University), and Clemson University. They motivated me beyond their classroom lectures by the personal understanding and support they continually gave. Their personal interest in me prompted me to do my best.

The three families I worked for during my college years were also very instrumental in my love and appreciation for life. All three families had special-needs children. In addition to each family's appreciation for my service, I was privileged to observe their ardent love for their severely mentally and physically challenged children. This helped me further understand God's love and His expectation of my love for all people regardless of their condition in life.

I cannot forget the support I have experienced in my workplace for the last twelve years. I am particularly grateful for the support of my supervisor, J.F.H. During an agency meeting, shortly after my hire, I was asked to give a verbal report of my work in the field. As a case manager with a caseload of at least fifty-two clients and many successful experiences, it should have been my privilege to report. Instead, without any warning, I was overcome by emotions of my childhood trauma. However, the smooth intervention of my supportive supervisor effectively took the edge off what could have been one of my most embarrassing moments. Thank you, J.F.H.

Indeed, my support system on my job has been a very important part of my life. My memories of L.K., my ex-supervisor, are very rich. I recall his words of encouragement upon my return from my Certified Addiction Counselor's (CAC) written exam. He informed me of his prayers on my behalf during his church service the day before the exam, which was very inspiring. He also encouraged me to have more faith in my abilities when I was just sure I had failed the exam because of one difficult section.

I am also very thankful for my supportive ex-supervisor, J.W., who despite his overwhelming schedule always took time out to take a listen to me.

My last ex-supervisor, S.P., was also amazing. I had mixed emotions about his resignation—happy for his well-deserved accomplishment and regretful about losing him.

I appreciate each of my colleagues who bless my life every day. I am especially thankful for my two coworkers with advance computer skills. I never felt the need to inform them about the reason for my below college-level computer proficiency because they never inquired. K.B. and C.W., I am much obliged. I know I've said it before, but please, hear it again: I could not have made it without your assistance. S.C., my prayer warrior and strong motivator for courage and faith, I love you for it. I sincerely pray that God will answer your mother's prayer. C.W. and J.J., don't forget I need to meet with your mothers about my very important question. To my two new coworker neighbors, C.S. and R.F., I appreciate your laughter and listening ears for my venting. M.D. and T.H., we share a common drift. My life is more fulfilled because of each of you. To M.M., thanks for knowing me so well.

I would also like to extend my thanks to my ex-coworkers. E.G., I'm glad that your leaving us did not result in your physical absence; I am glad I still have access to your smiles and hugs. C.E., B.M., B.T., B.C., R.R., R.W., D.G., P.N., A.Mc., K.L., and S.E., I am still cross that I couldn't hold back my tears when you left, but they were not only tears of sadness; they were tears of joy and appreciation for our very worthwhile, memorable times together. L.S., I miss your calling of my name—you pronounced my name meaningfully and cheerfully. R.R., and R.M., some of your inspirational e-mails and notes are secured in my inspirational collections but most importantly, in my heart. S.G., thanks for taking time to share with me your rewarding experiences in the field of human services. R.L., I now understand your reason for insisting that I take the last item you offered me. I will forever cherish it in your memory.

I am also obliged to extend appreciation to Horace Holloway and his wife, Jean; the late Eddie Jefferson and his wife; Eunice Sims; and Bessie Groves. My husband and I still appreciate the generosity of the Holloways, our landlord during our challenging residency in Belton City. Jean, although our meetings are now few and far between, your warm hugs and smiles every time we accidentally meet still resonate with me. Walter and Thomas Jefferson, because your parents are not here to receive my gratitude for sharing their garden with us, I consider you worthy of receiving their commendation. Besides, we do appreciate your "drop-by" visits. Eunice Sims, I consider you a very special, one-of-a-kind cosmetologist in that I did not have to tolerate the usual gossip of some beauty salons. Instead, I looked forward to our Christ-centered, life-enriching chats. In addition, despite my status of a random customer, you gave me special privileges, including calling you at your home to schedule my appointments at my convenience. Your kindness reminds me of the difference between services prompted by love for others versus services rendered for monetary gains only. Ms. Groves, I am convinced that the reason you no longer call is related to your senior moments and not to your heart, because you are yet to fail at recognizing my voice, which reminds you of my name. Your laughter still sounds like music to my ears.

To the many clients who speak words of appreciation and commendation into my life—I trust that I have done the same for each of you. Your ardent courage and resolve to make positive lifestyle changes, and knowing I helped influence such changes, remains one of the most gratifying, fortifying, and rewarding experiences of my life. You are another reminder that we are all fallen beings in a fallen world. Yet, we are not destined to unending consequences of doom, because the God who knows and loves us is in control of eternal life.

To one female client, thank you for reminding me that you are waiting to read my manuscript; I'm thankful not to disappoint you. To one gentleman client, you were one of my most effective motivators for completing this book. I apologize for the long wait.

Although I have only seen the following people on television, their contributions to my life are very important. In fact, my biggest motivation for sharing my life experiences resulted from viewing an episode of the Oprah Winfrey Show. The date was April 15, 2011. Because of my failure to document the details of the show, I am not able to recall it in its entirety. However, I do recall the inspiring guest and his impact on me. His name is Clayton, and he experienced several years of neglect and abuse. His story was more than my heart could tolerate. More than the painful thought of this young man's unimaginable, physical discomforts, were the disheartening thoughts of his painful, suppressed emotions as a child. It was horrible to imagine the intense trauma to the child's brain during his approximate six years of isolation in a bathroom closet and knowing that his father and stepmother were responsible for his discomfort. Secondary features of this show indicated Clayton's intervention by his nine-year-old stepsister, who, during the parents absence, risked her own safety by unlocking Clayton's closet and allowing him the luxury of a child's favorite meal—cereal and milk—at the table quite hurriedly. I tried to imagine Clayton's mixed emotions of thankfulness and fear that his parents would return soon. I wondered how this child survived such cruel torture, deprived of basic needs like play time, adequate nutrition, sunlight and fresh air, adequate human interaction, love, and the physical touch of family members. How was healthy brain development and physical growth possible? It was hard to believe that this handsome, poised, composed, and emotionally healthy young man had been through so much. What I admired most was his cheerful spirit and lack of bitterness and resentment. This inspired me so much. I am sure most of the painful emotions I felt just then were about Clayton's experience. The others were related to reminders of my own childhood trauma.

During this emotional show, I also experienced an inconceivable shock. While attempting to wipe off my tears, my right hand by some mysterious power was directed to my upper right forehead where

I felt a familiar lump—an unnecessary lump of flesh that had been absent for almost thirty-eight years and was not missed. In a panic, I rushed to the closest mirror. It was not a mistake or dream. It was a nightmare. A reflection of my face indicated an obvious lump in the very location of my initial tumor so many years ago.

"Oh dear God, please not again," I whispered, tears still gushing down my face. At that time, the tears were in response to my past painful experiences of surgeries, physical and emotional pain.

Once more I whispered, "Lord, not again."

Then, I heard an internal voice with the following explicit directive, "Finish the book."

"Yes, Lord," I responded. "By your grace and mercy, I will finish the book."

I was then able to return to the conclusion of the show. Clayton's sister, because of the condition of her home, decided to run away. The story's happy ending involved a police officer, relatively new on the job. Yet, his very wise, caring, dedicated, and persistent manner of intervention resulted in Clayton's rescue. He was placed in the care of a responsible and loving aunt. This happy ending was possible because some people cared enough to get involved and make a difference.

Until this moment, I considered myself a humble person willing to share and care, and to go above and beyond in response to anyone's cry for help. Yet, for the last two decades, I have postponed completion of this manuscript on the basis of what I believed was my God-given right to privacy. Considering the positive impact that many different people have had on my life, it is hard to believe I would not want to return this kindness. You see, beyond my good intentions I am still a fallen human, selfish, self-centered and self-protecting. That is not a God-given right. That is of the enemy—the self in me.

For years, I entertained the idea of writing a book." When Elder Sherrod asked me if I had ever considered it, I knew God was speaking to me through him. I eventually got started, but viewed every roadblock as an indication that publishing my life story was not God's will. Yet, sub-consciously, I knew I was making excuses. Several years after completing twenty-one chapters, I decided that was enough and contacted a publisher. Right after relinquishing the book to the publisher, I decided to pray more before finalizing the publication. During the following months and years, I ignored the publisher's offers for publication. One very impressive event gave a 50 percent reduction in price because of a grant available to the publisher that I thought would be good. Still, I procrastinated.

Years later, I felt inspired to add couple chapters and submit the manuscript for publication. Unfortunately, by then my floppy disk was very outdated, and I had difficulties locating a computer service to convert the old disk to a current format. In addition, for reasons too complicated to explain, the only hard copy of the book was lost and never found. So, again, I considered it a wasted effort because it was not God's will. I know, now, that the problems I incurred in bringing this book project to completion were all related to my self-centeredness.

Once convinced of my problem, I prayerfully re-engaged in the project. This time it would not be my book project. Instead, I saw it as an opportunity to reach and bless others who might need encouragement to move beyond past failures. Whether by their own choosing, by inherited tendencies, by environmental influences, or a combination of all three, I can relate. I too was stuck in my circumstances until the hands of God, through human agents, reached my trembling, feeble hands and raised me up to stand on Christ the solid Rock. All my life I perceived I was born for a specific purpose. What better purpose can be mine than caring for others?

After I was convicted to publish the book once more, the project still did not come easily. However, I remained persistent. After much prayer, I found a company in Greenville, approximately one-hour roundtrip from my home, who assisted with converting most of the old floppy to a current disk. The company was there all along, but I was too focused on making up excuses to pray about the roadblocks. Of course, as we already know, the enemy shows up more forcefully when a person is within God's will. I was no exception. The legible contents of the new diskette included up to chapter fifteen. After several unsuccessful attempts by two computer shops to rewrite the illegible six chapters, not to mention the extended monetary cost, I was inspired to re-write the missing chapters. To my surprise, I did not know what to write about in them. As a result of prayer and the works of several artists mentioned in the book, I was inspired to include the chapters about my teen pregnancy, the "Forgiveness" chapter, and the chapter about my husband's police brutality.

Although desiring and praying for total surrender to God, the enemy of self remained vigilant. At times, I feared the ridicule that might happen because of my failures. Other times, I feared some would consider me as coward and co-dependent, or attention seeking. My most fearful concern relates to my role as a substance abuse counselor. I wondered what my clients would think if they read the book, and if they would begin to question my abilities. I thank God for His Holy Spirit, for soundness of mind, and for the cognitive ability to choose God's will over selfish desires.

Once convicted to do it God's way, He continued to show up in diverse ways mostly through other human beings. For example, on March 15, 2013, as I concluded the last chapter of the book I was faced with these aforementioned fears of negative criticisms. I took a break and began working in the kitchen. I turned on the radio and was blessed with a very pertinent message on my favorite Christian station from Toccoa Falls College. The presenter's main topic was about God allowing us victories or just abilities to cope with the worst of our life's dilemmas, in order to reach out and bless others faced with identical or similar experiences. The speaker seemed to be speaking directly to me.

Hearing him speak, I was convicted of my desire to fit into God's will and purpose for my life. This ideal reminds me of the strong conviction that was my experience during my new-birth conversion. I was twenty-one years old. Stepping out of the baptismal pool, the life, death, and resurrection of Christ and God's plan of the new earth and everlasting bliss with the heavenly host was so real to me that I momentarily thought, *Lord, if my death would result in salvation for another, I will gladly die.*

I did not understand the true meaning of this thought, because days later, and other times along the way, I tremble to think that I considered my death worthy of another's salvation. Who would dare cherish such a thought? Who in their right mind dares to think his or her life is worthy of another's salvation? There is only one life worthy of our redemption, and I know it is not my life. So, to what could I attribute this seemingly, self-exalted thought?

The answer was one of my spiritual breakthroughs realized during the progress of this manuscript. I gratefully announce it is unrelated to my physical death and definitely related to my death to self.

So then, last, but by no means least: I thank God for allowing me to reach this place of progress, realizing that the only true meaning to my life is contingent on my love for God and for others. It is my innate core value to love others with the kind of love that is only possible when one is connected to the true Source of love. Because of His self-sacrificial love unto the most cruel, most debilitating death, we as humans can access the blessed hope of eternal life with Jesus. It is this blessed hope that keeps us anchored in the storms for personal and intrapersonal lessons that guide us to soundness and wellness of body, mind, and spirit. So, while I am not worthy of emulating such a sacrifice, I am thankful for an opportunity to share my life story.

At this point, my greatest fear is that I have failed to extend appreciation to one or more persons whose influence has impacted my life positively through the storm. If so, I apologize and plead that you charge it to my brain but not to my heart.

(With the proceeds of this book, I hope to provide additional support for the mental disorder population including those with traumatic brain injury).

We invite you to view the complete
selection of titles we publish at:

www.TEACHServices.com

Scan with your mobile
device to go directly
to our website.

Please write or email us your praises, reactions, or
thoughts about this or any other book we publish at:

TEACH Services, Inc.
P U B L I S H I N G
www.TEACHServices.com ● (800) 367-1844

P.O. Box 954
Ringgold, GA 30736

info@TEACHServices.com

TEACH Services, Inc., titles may be purchased in bulk for
educational, business, fund-raising, or sales promotional use.
For information, please e-mail:

BulkSales@TEACHServices.com

Finally, if you are interested in seeing
your own book in print, please contact us at

publishing@TEACHServices.com

We would be happy to review your manuscript for free.

CPSIA information can be obtained
at www.ICGtesting.com
Printed in the USA
FFOW05n1917181114